T0104000

MEMOIRS
— OF —
GLOBETROTTERS

TENGKU HALIMAH SALIM

Order this book online at www.trafford.com
or email orders@trafford.com

Most Trafford titles are also available at major online book retailers.

© Copyright 2016 Tengku Halimah Salim.
All rights reserved. No part of this publication may be reproduced, stored in a
retrieval system, or transmitted, in any form or by any means, electronic, mechanical,
photocopying, recording, or otherwise, without the written prior permission of the author.

Print information available on the last page.

ISBN: 978-1-4907-7291-2 (sc)
ISBN: 978-1-4907-7292-9 (e)

Because of the dynamic nature of the Internet, any web addresses or links contained in
this book may have changed since publication and may no longer be valid. The views
expressed in this work are solely those of the author and do not necessarily reflect the
views of the publisher, and the publisher hereby disclaims any responsibility for them.

Any people depicted in stock imagery provided by Thinkstock are models,
and such images are being used for illustrative purposes only.
Certain stock imagery © Thinkstock.

Trafford rev. 04/22/2016

Trafford
PUBLISHING® www.trafford.com

North America & international
toll-free: 1 888 232 4444 (USA & Canada)
fax: 812 355 4082

Memoirs of Globetrotters

Contents

A Quote to Remember

"Don't write your name on sand, waves will wash it away

Don't write your name in the sky, the wind will blow away

Write your name in hearts of people you come in touch with

That's where it will stay."

To Rosy, Nor, May, Raihana, Maryati, Nora, Doris, and Marie who helped me write this book, and my deepest appreciation for their trust in me.

I wish to dedicate this book to the characters of *Memoirs of Globetrotters* for bravely agreeing to expose their life stories to be published without as much as using fictitious names. I thank them for having faith in me to write about their life and experiences in foreign lands, which in my opinion will be interesting to the readers in their motherland as well as the countries that they have adopted.

About the Book

In *Memoirs of Globetrotters*, I write about Asians who have made lives in other countries other than their own; viz. America, England, Australia, Italy, and Malaysia. Some have left their mother country from an early age following their families on diplomatic postings. I also touched on life in the diplomatic world, which I found interesting and which I feel would be interesting to the readers. I also wrote on places, some remote, some familiar to readers, which were their hometowns before they left to venture to faraway places. Their experiences as a foreigner are all mentioned as part of their life overseas. Most of these events happened as far back as in the 1950s. I have categorized the characters under three different groups; viz.: Children of Diplomats, the Missionaries and the Adventurers, based on their life stories and experiences. All the stories are true and some heart breaking, and they touch on the path of life through the choices they made, their own or chosen for them.

My characters are real and I choose them from different walks of life. A few are very close to me, and when I wrote about them, it was as if I knew a certain part of their life already. Others are people I have met in my life and became friends, and I chose them simply because I find their life fascinating and their personalities different and interesting. I would term them as my "characters" as I was curious as to how they coped with their life being on their own away from their familiar surroundings, how they managed to make it in a foreign land, and their aspirations in life.

This book is about life. The lives of the people close to me and who have faith in me to tell their story. When I told them that I wish to write about their lives, initially they found it flattering until doubts began to set in as the whole world will know about their life. Then again, my characters are people of strength and wisdom, having gone through the perils of life as they had. Their lives are different but never dull. I hope the reader will enjoy this book as it relates to many of us, our peers and families.

Prologue

When we were children, we hadn't a care in the world what was to become of us. Our happiness was to have a family and food and to be able to play our childish games. When we became adults, we often wondered of our future and wished for the crystal ball to transform us into what we wished to become while some have to struggle through life only to be rewarded later, sometimes in a better future or afterlife. I grew up believing in "qadar" and "qadho," Muslim terms that mean God the Almighty had already chartered our life for us. The path had already been predetermined in the palm of our hands, for which astrologists have tried for centuries to study the fine lines in our palm in order to find the secret answer. Marriage is regarded as the key to our future, which sometimes changes our luck in life just like in the fairy tale of Cinderella and her prince who came to rescue her. Whatever decision at this romantic moment of our life that we choose is the answer and the path of life we have chosen for ourselves. Trials and tribulations are only a test of our perseverance and acceptance of our choice, only to be rewarded in later life, maybe not materially but spiritually, because happiness can only come through one's own contentment.

I have come to a conclusion too that people are the same regardless of their origin. Our color or status in life may influence our lifestyle and thoughts due to our upbringing and childhood. Nevertheless, we all want happiness, material comfort, and a happy family. This is our basic comfort zone before we venture to have an ambition, which is to be recognized and to have material wealth, which will be our goals in life to achieve. If we were to look back on our childhood, we remember that we were more open to friendship and it did not matter to us who were our friends as long as they made us happy.

Our friends who have travelled all over the world have found this similarity among them in their choices in life as they dared themselves to take the first step in an unfamiliar ground. They discovered that people are the same everywhere even though their way of life might be different. It is the same fear of rejection and wanting to be accepted that matter to everyone. But once that has been conquered, one will find that it is just as easy to relate to a foreigner as it is to one's own people as long as both are on the same wavelength. So if one does not find happiness in one's home ground, the world is yours to conquer. So let us not be judgmental of anyone's choice in life, because when one is at that vulnerable stage of one's life, love plays a very important part. For many years people have pondered on the mysterious word "love," which sometimes cause havoc on many human beings, young and old. They become restless, unreasonable, and unexplainable when confronted with this special feeling.

The radio played love songs endlessly, while movies make millions of money on love stories with happy or not so happy endings. Remember the sad ending of Scarlet O' Hara and Rhett Butler in the blockbuster movie *Gone with the Wind*, how we wish we could rewrite the ending. Many poets have written many romantic poems on love, including many from Lord Byron and Samuel Butler.

"Through perils both of wind and limb
Through thick and thin she followed him."
—Samuel Butler

"It's better to have loved and lost than never to have loved at all."
—Samuel Butler

"To live is like to love
All reason is against it.
And all healthy instinct for it."
—Samuel Butler

"There is a lady, sweet and kind
Was never faced so pleased my mind
I did but see her passing by
And yet I love her till I die."
—Thomas Ford

Life is indeed a mystery to which only God the Creator knows the answer. The only solution for us is to take stock of our life at some juncture, realize our happiness or unhappiness, change our path of life when it is not too late, or accept life as being destined for us and make the best of it. And we could be spiritually happy because, as I said earlier, happiness only comes through our own contentment in life. Some people go through life without questioning and instead accept both the good and the bad, which is also a blessing as they say ignorance is bliss. Take for instance the individual characters mentioned. Each person has their own path of life to follow and make good of what was chosen for them.

Chapter 1

THE EARLIER DAYS
OF DIPLOMATS

"A steady patriot of the world alone
The friend of every country but his own."
—Anonymous

It was my childhood dream to be able to see places, foreign places you only see in the new geographical magazines and books that you read. To be received by dignitaries and assimilate with the dignitaries of every foreign land that you visit. We heard of the richness of the Ottoman Empire, the Blue Mosque, the Topkapi Palace where the sultan resided, and the caves at Cappadocia; the famous pride of Turkey, the Bhosporus River, which connects Turkey to Eastern Europe. I read every book I could catch hold of that relates to the high life of a diplomatic circle.

I was utterly spellbound by the legendary tales and scandals of the imperial court. If only I had been born during those times to experience these true tales passed down from the predecessors and to hear stories of their experiences would have been so exhilarating, so strange, and so inexplicable to us. I imagined witnessing the coronation of Tsar Nicholas in 1826, and enjoying the festivities of being in Peking some fifty years later in the heart of the Forbidden City itself and have tea with the Chinese Dowager Empress Tzu Hsi like Mary Fraser did. I read about the experience of 100 diplomatic women in Daughters of Britannia within the lifespan of 350 years of history, from the glittering social whirl enjoyed by Countess Granville in Paris to the not as fortunate sufferings of a certain Catherine MacCartney at the turn of the century, who in her seventeen years at Kashgar in Chinese Turkistan saw only three other European women.

In the sixteenth century, it was said that the idea of sending a resident ambassador abroad was fairly new and it was listed in treaties and manuals that this person chosen "to lie abroad for the good of the country" should have a long list of attributes. I quote, a diplomat should not only be tall and handsome, well born and blessed with a sweet voice and a well sounding name, and should also be well read in literature, in civil and canon law, and all branches of secular knowledge, in mathematics, music, geometry, and astronomy. He should also be able to converse elegantly in Latin tongue and be a good orator. He should have good morals and be loyal, brave, temperate, prudent, and honest and all the attributes fit for a diplomat.

As for the diplomatic wives, one of the most important role is to be able to assimilate in the social life and entertain well. She must also be a good cook, as an embassy wife's role in the culinary process is all important even in the grandest embassy household where there are numerous domestic staff. It would be an invaluable help for embassy wives to be able to host for up to 250 people and help the chef and the kitchen staff, as well as stand in for them in case of emergencies. Another important role is to be able to supervise the domestic staff of different nationalities. After the lengthy and often laborious process of buying, preparing, and cooking the food, the method of training the waiters was a despairing subject. At certain times, if necessary, the only solution was to ask for the comradeship of one of the diplomatic sisters to help for a special sit-down, important dinner party, to oversee operations from the kitchen like heating up dishes, serving out, and thrusting wines and rolls into the maids' hands. To quote a diplomat's wife at Ulan Bator in Mongolia, once at a dinner party hosted by her husband the ambassador, Brigitte recalled that when seated at the table her anxieties were far from over for in spite of her coaching the waiters were fond of getting in each other's way and occasionally there were unseemly wrangles between the headwaiter and the masterful butler who would sometimes wrench the bottle of wine from the headwaiter in order to fill up the guests' glasses.

In another incident, it was reported that once at another posting in Africa, at a dinner party hosted by the same diplomatic couple, Bridget Keenam and her husband, their butler Caesar disappeared. The plates needed clearing away and Caesar was not to be seen for some time. The ambassador whispered, "Caesar," louder and louder, getting a bit desperate. Suddenly Caesar was back at his side. The ambassador asked in an undertone, "Caesar, where have you been?" Caesar innocently and smilingly replied to the appalled guests, "Sorry, Boss, I went for a pee." Trying to make a joke out of it, Keenam said laughingly, "Well, I hope you washed your hands." To which Caesar replied, "Oh no, Boss," indignant that anyone would think he had wasted time rather than hurry back to continue his duty.

An earlier ambassador, Mr. John McNeil, had been a doctor before he joined the foreign service and was made ambassador to Persia before Vita. He had cured the shah's favorite wife and one of the children of smallpox. In return,

John and his wife Elizabeth were shown the affluent lifestyle in the Middle East and were invited to the royal harem. This was Elizabeth's detailed description of her visit and the splendor she witnessed.

"Myself led on a horse, dressed in white satin with broad lace flounces, my blue stones, etc., my outward garb was a great wide cloak of crimson silk lined with pale blue and a large calash of the same. You are aware that the point of a lad's finger even dare not be seen in Persia. I had three running footmen of my own before me."

Like the other diplomatic women who were granted this rare privilege, once inside the. royal harem Elizabeth was almost overcome by the opulence of the scene that greeted her.

Nothing could exceed the splendor, the magnificence, the dazzling richness, and brilliance of the scene. The slave girls were in diamonds and rubies, brocade, and spangles. Their dresses, originally of the richest stuff, were so closely embroidered with pearls and precious stones that little else could be seen. Their hair hung loose, and their heads were ornamented in various ways with jewels. The queen sat on a crimson velvet cloth richly embroidered with pearls, and reclined against a large square cushion of the same material, with the only difference that the pearls here were so close together as to leave almost no portion of the velvet visible. Her own dress was most magnificent. The precious stones alone cost, independent of setting, about £150,000, which made her gape with disbelief!

On the niche above her head was placed the crown of the Shah, an exquisite thing, and on each side of it a black Persian lamb skin cap ornamented with sprays of the largest diamonds. Beside her lay the famous armlets of the Shah, in one of which is the diamond called "the Sea of Light." In the various other niches were candlesticks, dressing materials, basins, and caskets, all of the best precious stones and purest gold.

Who would be more familiar or well informed of a new country or place if not through a diplomat's life where one is able to mix with the locals or natives? Algiers might have seemed to appear inconspicuous and distant to a foreigner, but only after assimilating oneself with the locals and adopting their lifestyle could one discover that the Europeans in Algiers were always well dressed and elegant, more so than in London, and the women dressed similar to the fashion from *Le Journal Des Modes*. The wife of the British consular in Algeria was struck by the beauty and courtesy of the Algerians and the opulence of the Algerian women.

Life in Algiers was indeed delightful. Although the consular corps was a small close-knit community, it was large enough to provide an ample supply of balls, dinners, banquets, and masques. The biggest spectacle for her was when she paid a visit to the Dey's wife herself. As the wife of a British consul, she was considered an important visitor, and the Dey's women took the greatest possible care over their preparations. They made ice sherbets of orange flower water, together with vast quantities of different foods—meat, poultry, pastries and sweetmeats—which she ate with beautiful rosewood spoons, their tips inlaid with amber and coral. She learned the art of sitting comfortably cross-legged on the floor with the other women in Moorish fashion, and every comfort had been thought of. The table on which the food was set was inlaid with silver jugs, exquisitely embroidered napkins were brought for her to wipe her hands on.

Entertainment is only one aspect of a diplomat's life, which involves wining and dining and being entertained in return. Awesome stories of diplomat's wives being entertained became widespread rumors about the lavish life being lived by the diplomat and his spouse abroad. One such story was quoted in the memoir of one of the diplomats' wives when she was invited to the wedding of the chief judge's or "cadi's" daughter in Algeria. "My eyes were perfectly dazzled by the splendor of the jewels by which their 'salamas' or capes and persons were covered, whole bouquets of roses, jasmines, peacock feathers and butterflies were completely formed of diamonds." The bride herself was so bedecked with jewels that she was quite unable to bear the weight of her *salama* or cape without the support of her two attendants, who walked on either side of her and held her head. She wore so many rings in her ears that her ears were quite bent down, hanging in the elephant style. On her arrival at the palace harem, not only the women but also the whole room was heaped with jewels. There were jewels spread out over the tables and shelves, and there were even jewels on the floor— emeralds, sapphires, and rubies, which seemed to grow up out of the cut-velvet carpets like so many fantastical flowers. It was like a dream, a dreamlike experience Elizabeth will not forget in her lifetime.

Despite the glamorous life and privileged access to the royal houses and when the ambassador is accredited, it is not always enviable when it becomes a regular official duty.

To quote a not as pleasant experience from a diplomat's wife, every Thursday in Vienna is when the wives of ambassadors were expected to call upon the grand maîtresse. On this solemn occasion, no tea was served and the conversation had to be general and utterly impersonal touching only on three interesting subjects; the imperial family, politics, and gossip being tabooed.

At court balls, the emperor and empress made their way into the white ballroom with the imperial family to preside over the evening's entertainment. The women would be ablaze in silks and diamonds, and the men in outlandish Austrian uniform. The room itself, lit by one thousand candles, was one of the most beautiful she had ever seen, remarked one diplomat's wife, although such evenings were exhausting as there were no refreshments served. And everyone had to stand all night until she was close to fainting, recalled another wife. There are times even today when public life as a diplomat's wife seems to require almost impossible levels of stamina in order to cope.

There have also been stories of hardships and compassion faced by the predecessors, such as the compassionate Blanckleys in Algiers, who had housed fifteen Englishmen who had been shipwrecked on the Barbary Coast and captured by local savages. Mrs. Blanckley took them under her care, caring for them and tending to their wounds and overfeeding them after their long state of starvation.

In 1947, when a diplomat's family arrived in Baghdad during the ferocious heat, to their disappointment they found that their house had no curtains and no furniture, and worst of all, no fridge or fans. The office provided them with an allowance with which they had to buy everything themselves.

On the contrary, life in the diplomatic world was not always a bed of roses, especially if they were sent to the most remote countries, such as Kashgar, which was a tiny flyblown oasis settlement on the western fringes of the Taklamakan Desert, to represent the interests of the handful of British Indians, mostly small- time traders living there. Life in Kashgar was always tough and often very lonely, and for the first eight years George had only one European friend there, who was a priest with whom he was able to converse in their only common language, which was Latin.

One of the hardship posts was to China during the Cultural Revolution. To quote a diplomat stationed there during that time:

> "We had no contact with the Chinese whatsoever. They weren't allowed to even say 'Hello' to us on the street and our neighbours weren't allowed to be neighborly. One day, the teacher who was teaching me Chinese language, was giving a great tirade against the ghastly imperialists, although I could not understand a word of it."

He was saying all the horrible things about the English and Americans. It was not until twenty two years later, long after he retired that they were able to speak to one of the neighbors.

When Mary Fraser followed her husband to Peking, the British legation in Peking served as a refuge from a hostile outside world. She regarded Peking as enormous and a sanctuary after paying courtesy calls at other legations. She was acutely aware that the streets outside, for all their squalor and poverty, were full of enemies. The Chinese had held for nearly half a century against giving full diplomatic representation to European countries and therefore, as foreigners, diplomats were detested figures, especially the British because of the hostility fueled by recent events. Mary chose seclusion and was content to remain surrounded by the immense and impregnable wall as the legation was a little world in itself. Mary used to write grim tales of cruelty floated over the walls to us. The principal building in the compound was the residence of the envoy and his wife, its wooden beam painted in Chinese style in the richest peacock greens and blues and gold.

When another diplomat was posted to Benghazi in Libya, the English couple was daunted by the conditions under which they were expected to live, especially after leaving their beautiful house in South Kensington in London. For Florence

Old, who arrived in Syria for the first time in 1983, she had to go to four different shops to get breakfast as there was no coffee nor jam nor butter in any one shop. In Communist countries like in Peking, they were not allowed to move more than a twelve-mile radius from the center of Peking. In the Soviet Union in the early 1960s, Ruth wrote that she felt their house was being bugged and whenever her husband wanted to say anything pertaining to individuals in the embassy they had to go for a walk in the botanical gardens.

Back in England, there was increasing criticism on the perceived extravagance funded by the taxpayer for diplomatic entertainment. It is the picture of an inbred group of people, cushioned from the hardships that beset the rest of humanity, regularly drinking duty-free liquor in each other's homes, which critics of diplomatic entertaining sometimes conjure up and was written in a book called *Handbook on Diplomatic Life Abroad*. A gruesome picture was painted of the diplomatic social scene in Mongolia in the 1970s. At all functions here, senior wives were treated like puppets, rigidly segregated, condemned to spend long hours discussing their children, the weather, and their imaginary illnesses (illnesses caused by being overweight and boredom). Ambassadorial dinners never included Mongolians and other staff, and were painfully formal and very long (five and six inedible courses are the general rule). In these elaborate social scenes, the wives of diplomats had acquired the technique of chatting brightly, saying, "Ghastly weather, isn't it?" and "Good time for the roses," over and over to different guests.

Although the excesses and the hardships during the early years are not as severe now or in recent years, still the life of the diplomat is the dream of every young person who enjoys a colorful life.

Chapter 2

CHILDREN OF DIPLOMATS

(a) A Malaysian Abroad

Diplomatic life, although intriguing, can also cause a lot of heartaches to the families involved because of having to uproot themselves from their homeland to a strange place. It is not just the physical acts of packing and unpacking, but also the mental frailty for the delicate Asian women. Many and varied are the difficulties that beset the wife of the diplomat when she first exchanges her life in the tropics to a new home in a cold country. The sudden and complete upset of old world life and the disturbance of long-existing associations produce in many women a state of mental chaos and incapacitates them. The interrupted schooling of the children disrupt their education and may cause insecurities in their later life. Rosy would be involved many times, not only in the preparations, which meant packing and unpacking, but also in the forthcoming departures, being the eldest and closest at hand. Although women were supposedly made of sterner stuff, the departures were often very painful upon realizing that one was going away for many years, away from family and good friends, and oblivious to the situation back home except through letters. Rosy's mother would tearfully wave her siblings goodbye as she was about to set off to her new life with her family and multiple luggage, which included many favorite foodstuffs and herbal remedies used to help in reducing joint aches and muscle pains, especially in cold countries.

My cousin Rosy is only a few years older than me as she was born only a day after my elder brother was born. They were both born in the same house where I grew up with the big, extended family of my maternal grandmother. I remember her always being my elder sisters' playmate while I was her younger sister's playmate. Only once in our childhood days do I recall being her playmate, and being authoritative she told me not to talk to one of our cousins. She was seven years old then and I was four years old, and I obeyed her as I was younger. Through the years, we saw each other from time to time and I always remember her as being my beautiful and sophisticated elder cousin. She didn't take much notice of me then when I stayed at her house during the holidays as I was her younger sister's friend. But I noticed her because she was different. She was special, unlike my other cousins, who were normal and ordinary. She appeared to have just come out of a fashion magazine. Every morning when I woke up during my stay at her house in the same room where we slept, I observed from my bed, which I shared with my younger cousin Noni, how she would backcomb her hair religiously while stiffening it with a lot of hairspray in order to turn it into a nice round "bob." Only then would she put on her school uniform to go to school. I used to see her sewing her own dress to go to a party, and more often, it was a top to match her many colored leggings. She created fashion. Rosy was a teenager then and very much into herself and she paid a lot of attention to the way she looked. In the evenings, she would be ready to go to a party with her grown up friends who would come to the house to fetch her, while Noni and I played indoor games and found ways to amuse ourselves. She was hardly home, and if she was in the afternoons after school, she would be talking and giggling on the telephone for hours on end, with her friends on the other line. Rosy was always in a world of her own!

Rosy was born beautiful and her name came from the word "rose," which is a nice, fragrant flower, a typical Malay name given to daughters. Born into an affluent family, she inherited her mother's and grandmother's good looks, a nice jawline and high cheekbones, deep-set eyes, and a sharp, pointed nose uncommon for Asians. Her mother admitted that Rosy's

Caucasian nose was the result of her habit of putting her thumb into Rosy's mouth and pressing it against the upper inside of her mouth, learned from her mother. It is commonly said among the Malay community that a pointy nose is a sign of shrewdness in business, which proved useful to her in later life. Rosy loved to giggle, and her confident manner as well as her well-spoken acquired English made her friends in awe of her. She stood five feet four inches tall, which in those days was uncommon for an Asian girl, and was as slim as a rake and wore her hair styled in a "bob" just like the actress Barbara Streisand, whom she admired. Rosy was also very vain and meticulous and would apply her make up flawlessly just like a makeup artist would. She was always up to date with the latest fashion and sewed her own clothes, a talent she adopted from her mother. She could capture her audience for hours with her gift of gab, and almost everyone would be captivated by her as she could be as charming as she could be obstinate and headstrong.

Rosy came from a privileged background. Her paternal grandfather was a wealthy landowner and her father was the eldest of four boys and two girls. He was the most studious and brightest of his siblings and received his secondary education at the prestigious Malay boarding school for boys in the northern state of Malaya. Her mother also came from a noble background and they were related to the royal houses of the eastern states of Malaya. Rosy was born in a small palace where her mother was staying temporarily with her grandmother and stepgrandfather while her father was away in England on a study course. However, the only recollection she had of the eastern state where she was born was that of the heat beneath her feet, possibly because of walking without shoes in her childhood days. She left her hometown at four years old to follow her parents to Kuala Lumpur and then later to the northern state of Perlis where her father was later transferred, going back to her maternal grandmother's house occasionally for visits. She recalled living with eighteen people in her house in Perlis where her father was taking care of his siblings as well as her adopted sister's family.

Rosy's recollection of her early childhood in Malaya was very vague as at the age of eight years old she left Kuala Lumpur for Australia with her parents as her father was posted to Canberra to work at the Malayan Embassy. She had a tough life growing up in Australia as she was labelled as being an aborigine because of her tanned complexion. She was the only Asian in the school and it was her first encounter with racism in her life. It did not help much that her father was very strict and disciplined and she had to walk to and from school every day and was teased by the Aussie children. Her father would not allow her to be chauffeured to school as he believed that the official car was only for his official use. When her parents later went to their second posting in Washington, DC, she was left behind in Canberra for a few months under the care of a Malaysian guardian in order to finish her piano lessons, which her father encouraged her to play well. Sadly, she did not excel in her music lesson and flew by herself to Washington, DC, to join her parents, who had moved from their first house to Rock Creek Park, their second house. Her father's position as a counselor at the Malayan Embassy made it necessary for her to participate in the embassy's social activities, and being the eldest daughter, to help her mother in her social activities. She took part in various social events like dancing, singing, and doing creative arts, and also helped her mother in the preparation of Malay food during the Eid festival known as "Hari Raya" and Malaysia Day celebrations.

She was enrolled in an American school when she was eleven and a half years old and discovered that American girls were a little too grown up for her age, but she learned to put on makeup just the same as the other American girls. She would put on her lipstick just like her schoolmates did and rub it off just before going home. Once again she had to learn to walk to school and back or went by bus like the local American children, as her father's policy was that as a representative of Malaysia all privileges, including the car and driver, were only for his use. In school Rosy gained another year because of the American schooling system. Moving from Australia to America and back again to Malaysia upset her education and cause her to eventually graduate at eighteen years of age, a year or more older than her contemporaries, which disturbed her. Returning to Malaysia made her lose a grade. The constant changing from English to American then English system again took a toll on her ability to catch up with her counterparts in the various countries she was in, but finally she graduated in Bangkok, Thailand, at eighteen years of age.

Rosy's mother, affectionately called "Aunty," did not receive English education at school but learned to pick up English language during her years abroad. Being a sociable lady by nature and coming from an affluent background, she saw the mixing of the British with the Malay officers at the social events hosted by her mother and stepfather, who held an important position as a Chief Minister of an eastern state in Malaya. Through her observation of her mother's experience with the British while she was young, she assimilated well with the foreign dignitaries while her husband was serving in the foreign service. She loved her duty as a diplomat's wife, and as she was brought up in a royal household with plenty of servants, it was natural for her to be able to handle them.

Incidentally, during her time, a foundation of Foreign Service Wives Association was formed in November 1960 and a talk was given, entitled in a no-nonsense way "Serving Abroad" and sent by newsletter to all the foreign officers' wives to remind them what was expected of them abroad. Coping with servants' problems remain one of the more complicated tasks faced by diplomatic wives. It became news and was reported that while in Santos the wife of a well- known international celebrity turned ambassador was forced to have no fewer than five sittings for each meal in her household. The first for Richard and herself and their guests, then it was followed by one for her Irish maid, who had been elevated from plain Mary to "Doña Maria," and her brother. Then, again followed by her German servants' dinnertime because they would not sit down with her black servants, who in turn would not sit down to dinner with the slaves, who were obliged to stand or sit in corners, where they were given "leftovers" or "leavings." It was said that dealing with staff in Muslim countries often carried an additional penalty clause as many male servants consider it demeaning to take orders from a woman, and so wives found that they had to fight to maintain any kind of authority in their own household. In Saudi Arabia, the wives were advised never to give orders but to request the jobs she wanted done. There was also a case of a Chinese servant who refused point-blank not only to take orders from her lady employer, but also serving her at the table on the grounds that the lady did her own cooking and could not therefore be a real lady.

Fortunately for Rosy's mother, she never encountered any of the problems above, having had the right training and experience of living with servants in her young days. Her warm personality charmed the whole diplomatic circle so much so that once her husband commented jokingly to Rosy in later years that lucky for him her mother did not pursue her education to a higher level, otherwise she herself would have become the diplomat.

Rosy's mother was an only child of her mother with her second husband, who died while she was four years old, and she was brought up by her stepfather in a big household with other siblings. She learned to love her stepfather like her own father, whom she never knew, and grew up being the eldest of her other siblings, except for her half-brother from her mother's first husband. When she turned into her teens and being the eldest girl, she frequently worried that she would end up as an old maid. Her mother dismissed her worries by getting her engaged and later to be married to her own nephew who was studying in a boarding school. They got married soon after he finished school at the Malay Boys College in Kuala Kangsar in the northern state of Malaya. While Rosy's father was a strict and conservative boy brought up by a strict and religious father, Rosy's mother was fun loving and enjoyed spoiling her children with clothes that she sewed herself. She was their supportive mother while her father was often strict and uncompromising. While young, Rosy misunderstood her father's strictness as noncaring, and became headstrong and rebellious toward him. It was only later after she got married and had her own children that she and her father understood each other and conversed with each other on any little subject at all.

After three years, her father's posting as a diplomat in Washington, DC, ended and they returned to Malaysia and she was enrolled in the all-girls' elite school on the west coast of Malaysia, named after the first queen of Malaysia. She made many friends in her new school who were captivated by her personality and her American accent and western way of life. She made many meaningful friendships that last to this day. Having been educated overseas and not having a good command of her own language, she did not do well in her Malay Language examination, which was a compulsory subject then, and had to leave the school. She then joined the Peel Road Convent in Kuala Lumpur to resume her studies before she left Malaysia again. During her parents' transfer to Kuala Lumpur, they lived in a comfortable wooden colonial-type house near the Lake Gardens, which was a prime residential area. She was sixteen years old and enjoying life as a teenager, and her western way and mannerism and her style of dressing became the envy and talk of all her friends. Most of her time was spent partying and socializing with her friends and her mother's friends and relatives, and because of her good looks and family background, she was well sought out by the Kuala Lumpur society. Looking back on her childhood, Rosy's favorite remark was that she was born a big fish in a small bowl.

After their short stay of barely two years in Kuala Lumpur, her father was again posted to Bangkok as the Malaysian ambassador to Thailand, a neighboring country. Rosy and her sister, Noni, tearfully left their beloved friends after having acquired many meaningful friendships and getting to know their country again. They left Malaysia. And while Rosy's father took up his new position as the new Malaysian ambassador, her mother played her role by involving herself in the hectic social life and duties. Rosy once again had to help her mother with her social work and even standing in for her mother to attend functions whenever her mother could not. She would even have to stand in for her parents' friends whose wife was not able to attend a certain important functions, such as "black tie dinners," and helped in the preparations for the Malaysia Day celebration and the Eid or Hari Raya celebration with the embassy staff. She attended the Ruam Rudy International School where children of diplomats and expatriates went, and met her soon-to-be best friend, Bonnie, whom she had met earlier in Kuala Lumpur and who was also to become a lifelong friend.

On that fateful day, Bonnie was meeting her boyfriend, Dickie, who invited his best friend Jack to join him at the school tuck shop with the intention of introducing Jack to Rosy. While still studying, Rosy was also doing photography modelling for various Thai fashion designers after school just to earn some extra pocket money. She enjoyed the job as well. It was just after she had graduated from high school and she was just eighteen, while Jack had just returned from the United States and was working in an advertising company. Jack fell in love with Rosy immediately upon seeing the beautiful Malaysian girl with a royal ancestry who spoke fluent English. But he was scared of her father, the Malaysian ambassador, whom he joked could put him in jail for dating his lovely daughter.

Jack came from a prominent Thai family and his parents divorced while he was two years old and was brought up by his maternal grandmother. His mother had mixed blood from Vietnam, Laos, and Thailand, and was a smart university graduate who lived most of her life in America after her divorce. Rosy's recollection of her father-in-law was that he was a very suave man, having spent much time in England, and very western in his mannerisms and ways. Rosy got on well with him as he used to show Rosy pictures of his ex-girlfriends, one of whom resembled Rosy. Her relationship with her mother-in-law, who she called Mami, was one of coolness although the latter adored her grandchildren. After spending a large part of her life in America, Mami moved back to Thailand and acquired a lot of land at the beautiful hillside resort of Chiang Rai. She died at a ripe old age of ninety-three.

After their first date, Jack wasted no time in courting Rosy, who was impressed by his thoughtfulness. After she graduated from high school, Jack gave her a mirror with lights as she was doing part-time modelling and had always been very vain about her looks. For her birthday, he bought her a lovely fabric after knowing that she loved to sew her own clothes. Being Asian and although educated in America, he disapproved of her micro-miniskirts and corrected her when she laughed too loud like a Westerner. Rosy was also enjoying the attention she received from some foreigners and also some admirers from her homeland, to Jack's dislike and which Rosy sometimes found to be a little too controlling. When Rosy introduced Jack to her mother, she was very happy that her headstrong eldest daughter had finally found a suitable Asian man to marry instead of a foreigner. She encouraged Jack to ask for Rosy's hand in marriage and arranged for him to meet Rosy's father. When Jack approached Rosy's father, during the conversation his pipe dropped to the floor in his surprise, as he had plans for Rosy to continue her education abroad. Rosy, he said, had just finished high school and was barely eighteen years of age. Jack left the house without getting his approval to marry Rosy. Meanwhile, Rosy's mother was distraught at the turn of events and asked for her good friend, a Malaysian lady from the embassy, to get the help of a religious man in order to have a special prayer for Rosy's father to reconsider his decision. Rosy's parents were at that time preparing to go back for their home leave to Kuala Lumpur for three months, taking the whole family with them. Rosy had given her uncle's address to Jack for him to visit her there after she left Bangkok as they had no forwarding address then. Jack, besotted by Rosy and afraid to lose her, approached his father to ask for a loan for a ticket to go to Kuala Lumpur to find Rosy and again ask for permission to marry her. When he arrived in Kuala Lumpur, he went to Rosy's uncle's house to ask for Rosy's father's address, and unknowingly, Rosy's uncle drove him to the house and left soon after. Rosy's father, after being cajoled by his wife, finally agreed to let Rosy marry this persistent young man. Jack and immediately arranged for a conversion for him to become a Muslim in order to marry Rosy. They were married at a mosque in Klang, after which Jack left Kuala Lumpur to go back to Bangkok, leaving Rosy still with her parents. Rosy was not allowed to follow Jack yet until they had a formal reception in Bangkok after her father's home leave. Rosy then spent time with her parents and followed them to a party at the home of a Malaysian royal at Frasers Hill.

Since her Malaysian relatives did not know about Rosy's sudden marriage to Jack, Rosy's mother received a proposal of marriage for Rosy, which she regretfully and graciously rejected. After their home leave, Rosy and her parents went back to Bangkok, where they held a wedding reception at the Malaysian Embassy, and only after the reception was Rosy allowed to live with Jack in their own house. Nine months later, Rosy delivered a little baby girl called Maya, followed by Lisa and Rita, who were born in Thailand. Just after they were married, Rosy's father was posted to Russia to resume his post as the ambassador in the USSR, and Rosy remained with her new family in Bangkok. She learned to adapt herself to her new lifestyle and adopted the Thai culture as her own. She spoke Thai fluently and worked as a public relations officer and announcer in their family cultural restaurant called "Baan Thai," speaking in English and Thai. With the help of a nanny and a Thai maid, she was able to run her family and household while at the same time participating in a children's clothing business with her sister-in-law, which they supplied to department stores. The Thai women were very industrious. For many years they had involved themselves in business, even though they appeared gentle in their ways and mannerisms. Rosy also started teaching English to young military students during the day and going to the restaurant in the evenings. With her flair for business and with an eye for beautiful jewelry, Rosy fitted perfectly with the lifestyle of Thai high society. She also got along well with her husband's family.

As we grew up and had our own families, Rosy and I were able to interact with each other. She would tell me about her life abroad and her trials and tribulations living in a Western country while bringing up her children with Asian values, which was not easy as the lifestyle was different and the people they saw from day to day were different from home. Seeing Rosy is not believing that her life had been a rollercoaster ride, because she was always well attired in elegant designer clothes, which were no longer sewn by herself, and with her expensive collection of jewelry, her well-chosen selection of designer shoes and handbags, her long habit of articulately made-up face, and lastly her permanently happy disposition, which made her company desirable. Not a trace of hardship was mirrored on her flawless face. After realizing all the traumas that she went through with Jack, such as the failed business venture in the beginning of her move to America, the death of her beloved brother whom she depended on and the demise of her beloved parents while she was away, and finally the devastating tsunami that claimed the life of her precious daughter and almost her own, Rosy must indeed have immense inner strength to weather the storm and accept her tragedies. It was, she said, her deep-rooted faith in religion that pulled her through without as much as a scar on her face and her inner self. Life is indeed a long journey and it is only God the Almighty who knows what is in store for us. To quote a saying by Nathaniel Hawthorne (1800–1864): "Life is made up of marble and mud."

Jack, the Entrepreneur

> "If a man begin with uncertainties, he shall end
> in doubts. But if he will be content to begin with
> doubts, he shall end in certainties."
>
> —Anonymous

Jack, after his return from America, worked as an advertising manager in an advertising company, and because of his artistic talent he won several awards from Switzerland. He then worked in the family carpet company and his creativity won him many renovation jobs at the old Imperial Hotel and other hotels in Thailand and a palace in Malaysia. However, being a born entrepreneur, he was not satisfied and yearned to have his own business that he started himself, even though he was already managing the family furniture business, manufacturing French reproduction furniture.

Jack's mother, who was then working with the United States Government in San Francisco, worried that Thailand would be taken over by the Communists after the fall of Vietnam and Cambodia, and persuaded Jack to move to America. Jack had earlier met an American businessman from Atlanta and they went into business together to export Jack's family's reproduction furniture to Atlanta and to market it from there to the rest of the continent. Jack was excited to try his luck in this land of opportunity and to follow his American dream. They moved to a simple house in Atlanta with the children and two Thai maids to help look after the children while Rosy helped Jack set up the business. Unfortunately, the American market did not favor the French reproduction furniture and they were not able to break into the American market. It was a difficult time for Jack and Rosy, especially as their American business partner was threatening them and almost going out of his mind with the failed business venture. Jack, in the meantime, was traveling from Atlanta to Bangkok and vice versa in order to source products to try for the American market and finally spotted silver and brass ornaments made in Thailand. He tried bringing the new ornaments to the North Carolina tradeshow and that became his lucky break. From then on, his fortune changed and he set up a factory manufacturing silver and brassware ornaments in the form of animals in Thailand and received bulk orders from Saks and Neiman Marcus, the two prestigious department stores in America. Since then, they never had to look back.

"If I have to sweep the streets of Atlanta, I would do it for my family." Those were Jack's words spoken in exasperation when his furniture business failed. Fortunately for him, he did not need to do so as his luck changed for the better. Having had enough of the manufacturing and the wholesale business, Jack decided to go into the property market. Jack had come across a piece of 168 acres of land belonging to a wealthy owner who had far too much more real estate than he could handle and was willing to sell to Jack for a song. Jack started building a few houses with his house on top of the hill at an area called Creekside Crossing on one hundred acres of land. Then he started work on another one hundred acres at Parsons Run. His third development was called Thornhill, consisting of two hundred acres of houses. It was not an easy beginning but his persistence kept him going. It was a rollercoaster ride for Jack, but as they say, each man is the architect of his own fate. Not a stranger to doing business in the east, Jack used the same tactic in public relations by knocking on the doors of his American neighbors, carrying a gift and introducing himself as the developer of the estate that he was going to build. He was also lucky that through his casual friendships with the elderly people who were owners of large plots of land he was able to buy from them at very reasonable prices. In time he developed 650 acres of land into his housing development and golf course called St. Marlowes. St Marlowes comprising of a clubhouse and golf course and upscale bungalow houses where Jack and Rosy lived with their growing family.

Jack's gifted talent in the development of golf courses and housing estates have earned him several awards in the community, and he was well known in the Atlanta community as a successful Asian developer. Besides receiving many awards for his developments, he also contributed to the wellbeing of the Atlanta community in cash and kind by donating land for a private school to be built, and helped to raise 1.4 million dollars for the school fund. His golf course was rated as one of the top thirty public and private golf courses. But nothing gave Jack more pleasure than to toil on his land, and he knew every nook and corner of his estate. His last development was called St. Ives, which comprised of 728 acres of land before he decided to return to his homeland to start a new venture as a hotel developer on his land at Khao Lak in Thailand.

Rosy, after the birth of her fourth child Tara, decided to stay home to bring up her children while leaving the business to Jack and her brother. Sidney, her younger brother, had come to work with Jack and Rosy just as soon as Jack had started his housing development and had been Rosy's extra arm and leg. Rosy enjoyed her life as a homemaker, taking care of domestic issues and seeing to the schooling of her children. She did not engage in many social activities as she preferred the company of her family and one or two special friends, among whom was her neighbor Dr. Lucille Jordan, an elderly sixty-three-year-old lady. Dr. Lucille came from a middle-class family from Houston. She worked with the Georgian education system, and had become Rosy's close friend and confidant. As is customary in Southern practices, each time a new family moved into the neighborhood they would be welcomed with food by the neighbors. As Rosy had been a working woman previously and later a housewife, busy with her domestic chores besides traveling twice or three times a year to visit her ailing mother, she did not care much for social life. She found the Americans whom she came in contact with to be more motivated with the dollar sign rather than being genuine friends. She also detected a certain feeling of racism among her peers in Georgia, and only concentrated on her only true friendship with Dr. Lucille, which lasted for thirty years. Dr. Lucille later died of Alzheimer's disease at ninety-three years of age when Rosy was in Malaysia, although Rosy did manage to speak to her on the telephone a few times before she died. Feeling her loss greatly, Rosy suffered another setback with the death of her younger brother Sidney, on whom she depended greatly since he came to America at her request to work with the company. Sidney, who left his beloved mother to move to America to help Rosy, married an American girl and had a daughter, and they became Rosy's closest family in Georgia until her elder brother Dean joined them later as the company grew bigger. Sidney, who was in his forties, contracted a viral infection and had gone to visit his ailing mother in Malaysia. After his return he was hospitalized and died a month after his own mother's demise. It was a terrible time for Rosy as Jack was at that time in Thailand attending to some business and she was left alone with her children. She was not familiar with the Muslim funeral rituals but luckily her daughter Rita managed to contact the nearest mosque. Upon going there, she met a nice Middle Eastern Muslim man who was standing near his long wheelbase limousine. When she told him her story, the nice man arranged for the funeral procession as it was a Friday and the Muslim men in that area went for their Friday prayers. Sidney was blessed that he was buried with full Muslim rites and prayers and a long procession of cars of strangers accompanying him to the graveyard and giving him a good funeral service, just as what would be done in his homeland by his family.

Jack's career in development took off despite some hurdles in his rollercoaster business. His final project was successfully launched with beautiful bungalow houses and an award-winning golf course. Rosy's elder brother Dean and Rosy's two daughters, Lisa and Rita, helped Jack with his new project wherever their help was required. Rosy was more free to visit her father back home after the demise of her beloved mother, and arranged for the wedding of her daughter Rita to Mark, a Taiwanese American graduate whom Rita met at the university. Jack and Rosy also became grandparents to Lisa's children. Rita had finished her studies at MIT and had been a bright student and an athlete like her father. She excelled in swimming, tennis, basketball, and golf besides being chosen by a Thai think-tank group to save money for the company. She was going for a promotion when asked by Jack and Rosy to help in the running of their estate so that she could relieve Rosy and enable her to travel more to Thailand and Malaysia. Jack had carved out a piece of real estate in order for Rita to build and sell her own houses and left the management of the estate to Rita, who Jack felt had the business ability to run it for him, which she did. Jack had already achieved his American dream while living in two countries, Thailand and America. Having completed what he had set out to do when he first arrived in America, which was to become an entrepreneur—the dream of millions of ambitious young people. He then decided to go back to his roots and set up a development on the land that he inherited through his family and which he himself acquired. America was also at that time hit by the subprime crisis that caused a lot of businesses to close. After months of playing golf and getting back into Thai society, Jack felt restless with the need to do something other than go into complete retirement.

He started to build a five-star hotel at Khao Lak, which was about two hours' drive from Phuket.

Rosy's youngest daughter, Tara, was born premature in 1977, weighing only four pounds. She resembled Jack and Rosy in her looks; her sweet face and sharp nose and tanned complexion were inherited from both parents. She was a quiet and demure child and dressed in an earthy fashion, more like a hippy than a fashionable daughter of rich parents. She was a great reader and devoured books faster than the average speed reader. Although she loved reading, she was not as interested in academics as she was in art, and was given a scholarship by the Georgian School of Art, the second best art school after the Rhode Island Art and Design School. But upon Rita's advice, she went to Rhode Island. After Tara finished college, Rosy decided to take a holiday to Italy together with Tara in order to visit Tara's half-Italian cousin Anastasia who was going to study law in the United Kingdom. The two cousins had a lovely time together and it was to be one of Tara's last family holidays.

It was during one of the family holidays when Rosy and the family gathered at their new hotel resort at Khao Lak and Tara went for a walk by the beach with the maid. Suddenly the maid saw a huge wave coming from a distance and pointed it out to Tara, who excitedly went up to the hotel to call her sister Maya to see the huge wave approaching.

"The Assyrian came down like the wolf on the fold
And his cohorts were gleaming in the purple and gold
And the sheen of their spears was like stars on the sea
When the blue waves roll nightly on deep Galilee."
—Hebrew hymn on the destruction of Sennacherib

"You could not see a cloud because
No cloud was in the sky
No birds were flying overhead
There were no birds to fly."
—Lewis Caroll 1832–1898

Rosy and Jack's estate in Atlanta

Chapter 2

CHILDREN OF DIPLOMATS

(b) The Tsunami

December 26, 2004, was a fateful day for Rosy and her family, unfathomed by anyone, although Jack had earlier received a telephone call from his friend in Bangkok who warned him to be careful that a tidal wave was expected along the Andaman sea. Rosy and Rita and Rita's husband Dick and their son were at the Penguin Club, which was the children's playhouse in the middle of the hotel's swimming pool. Tara had approached Rosy to tell her that she was going for a walk on the beach with the maid, while Maya, Rosy's eldest daughter, was in her villa. Jack had telephoned Rosy to warn her after receiving that warning from his friend. Just as soon as Rosy had put the telephone down, the lights clicked on and off and Rosy saw a cartoon like wave coming from the far horizon. She could not believe her eyes, thinking that the waves would not come so near the shore. Rita, on the other hand, was more alert and quickly told Dick to pick up the baby and run inside the hotel. Within seconds, the wave enveloped the room where Rosy was and the water level rose up so fast that it kept rising above her head and she was trying desperately to hold her breath.

Debris was everywhere and the children's toys and bicycles and furniture were floating in the water until Rosy could not hold her breath any longer and released it, thereby inhaling and sipping all the silt contained in the seawater while struggling to put her head above water. Suddenly, she felt someone pulling her up while the water receded and telling her to cling on to the wires, while at the same time she heard cries of a child calling, "Daddy, Daddy." The source of the voice quickly let go of Rosy in order to go to his child, who was left sitting on a ledge. As soon as he let go of her, a second wave came and Rosy fell into the water again and at that time she thought she was going to die. She remembered surrendering and saying to herself, "Oh, Allah, if I am going to die, please make it easy for me," and saying her last rituals. As soon as she said that, she felt a beautiful feeling and felt everything was easy, then the man's face reappeared to her and she was being lifted up again. She became conscious and said to him, "What is your name? I am the owner's wife." She was then helped by the hotel staff back into the hotel by using ropes made out of bedsheets for her to cling on.

In the meantime, Tara had gone for a walk by the beach with the maid. Suddenly the maid noticed an unusual scene. She saw water receding from the ocean and the whole scene was just the beach and the fishes were jumping out from the water. Tara quickly ran into the villa to tell her elder sister Maya to witness the scene, and just as she and Maya came out, they were suddenly engulfed by the furious tidal wave, sending Maya back in the direction of the hotel while Tara was swept away in a different direction toward the beach with the huge wave. Maya suffered many injuries on her back and had to be hospitalized for a month, while Tara was not found until three days later after a prolonged search. The entire Khao Lak village was in chaos as five thousand lives were claimed. Rosy and Rita went from corpse to corpse trying to identify Tara's body among the thousands of bodies in vain. After not being able to find Tara's body, Jack, stricken with grief, threatened to sell off the property. It was not until Rosy asked for the help of her cousin, Omar who was on his pilgrimage to Mecca to pray for them to find Tara's body that her body was found. Rosy recognized Tara's slim hands and soon arranged for her to have a Muslim bathing ritual. After asking two mosques, a third mosque, despite their heavy schedule, agreed to do the burial at Jack's property. Tara was buried with full Muslim rituals by the imam and his three followers and Rosy's family members at dusk at the property in the vicinity of the hotel, a special place reserved for her.

The whole gruesome experience somehow strengthened Rosy's spiritual being although there were times when she gave in to depression. After four months, she left Bangkok to go back to Atlanta to pick up the final pieces of her life there. She could not help but feel sad at the sight of the room formerly occupied by her only child born in America. The Atlanta community grieved with her and Tara's school gave their condolences in a special way reserved for those who have contributed a lot to society, especially Jack, who was their benevolent contributor, and they grieved with the family. The gruesome aftermath of the tsunami had left such an indelible mark on her that she needed psychiatric help in order to rid her of the shock of the tsunami and its toll on her family. For months after the tidal wave, she could not sleep as she imagined seeing many people around her whenever she opened her eyes. It occurred to her that it could have been the spirits of the dead people that she went around touching while looking for her daughter Tara. She made a brave step after she was feeling better, which was to go to the Holy Land, Mecca, to do her pilgrimage with her aunt accompanying her. It was due to her faith in God that she was able to go through each test miraculously. If you see Rosy now, one would never have imagined the hurdles that she went through. One only sees the success story of Rosy, the driving force behind Jack, a successful entrepreneur who had set out for America in search of his American dream. With success comes sadness, because as they say, "In life, there is no such thing as a free lunch." But to quote Rosy, life is a long journey, and if you think of the thousands of others who have lost their lives and belongings and their loved ones, they were lucky that they still have other children and their possessions. It was tragic but God the Almighty wanted the privileged to see the sufferings of the poor and only then could they be charitable. According to Islam, the rich had a duty to the poor, and Rosy, since the tsunami, had done away with material cravings. For every dollar that she spent, she gave away 10 percent to the poor. Jack took it upon himself to clean up the whole area of Khao Lak after the tsunami and the villagers were amazed whenever they came into contact with the "big man" in the neighborhood. Despite his prominent family tree, they saw only a simple man who went around the island in shorts and tee shirts and displaying the most humble nature. Very close to the hotel lay Tara's special place and Tara's tombstone was regularly visited by the family because just before the tsunami Tara had asked her sisters who were living in America if they were going to come back to stay in Khao Lak. Tara remained close to the family in spirit.

Rosy had always been a loner since young and immersed herself in books whenever she was by herself. Books were her source of information as the life of girlie lunches and prolonged chats bored her unless they were with her close friends or relatives. She loved doing things alone, which was not abnormal because half of her life was spent away from her people and in the company of strangers and she had learned to adapt herself to a different life from one that her peers were accustomed to.

Having gone through the ups and downs of her husband's business career and after losing her beloved daughter in the tsunami that she herself miraculously survived, nothing to her in life was a surprise anymore. She had always had a fear of water, and despite her home being by the beach, she was never one to spend time swimming in the sea or enjoy being in the sun like other sun lovers. Now as she stays in her beautiful Kartika residence in Chengrai amidst the picturesque forests of Thailand, where she could hear the birds singing in the trees as she wakes up in the morning, she thanks God for blessing her life. She would reflect on her life and was grateful that Tara was taken away at an age when she would not be corrupted or disillusioned by the real world, because Tara had always been an idealist. While in college, she was often astounded upon hearing of some of the lives of her peers, which was beyond her idealistic mind. Rosy, having submitted herself to the will of God the Almighty, believes that no one belongs to another but to God, who has the power to give and take. He had taken Tara because only He knows what is good for her. On reflection, just before Tara died she had painted a grayish portrait of herself that was different from her other radiant self-portraits. In this latest portrait was a rather pale-looking Tara with water underneath her. On another occasion, she had built a huge sand sculpture of a mermaid, which her father had noticed and commented on. She may have had a premonition of what was to come and it was meant to be. It might not be easy for many to cope with the loss of a beloved child, but being Rosy, who had endured life from a young age, this was just one of life's challenges for her. In her own psychoanalytical words, "Life is a long journey and it is not over yet."

Is she referring to the trials and tribulations of life contrary to the fairytale ending of "happily ever after" that we visualized in our youth?

Chapter 3

CHILDREN OF DIPLOMATS

(a) A Malaysian Girl in Italy

"So I have loitered my life away, reading books, looking at pictures, going to plays, hearing, thinking, writing on what pleased me best. I have wanted only one thing to make me happy; but wanting that have wanted everything."

—William Hazlitt

The sandy beaches of Adelaide are something to talk about. The waters are crystal clear, but in the middle of summer the temperature in the month of December could fluctuate to 20 °C. So apart from braving the chilly water, one also has to look out for the great white sharks that Australian waters are notorious for. As for dog lovers, the people of Adelaide seem to be caring humanitarians. Along the famous Gleneagh Beach is a strip of hotels beautifully positioned along the typical, older, intricately designed Australian houses that are becoming a rarity now as new streamlined buildings by famous Australian architects have become the main feature. At the end of the jogging track is a nice café serving Australian breakfasts of scrambled eggs and sausages and a nice aroma of brewed coffee where many, after the long walk, would welcome a hearty breakfast. The atmosphere is indeed very pleasant and sophisticated enough to be compared to the Cote d'Azur of France that the French are so proud of. The French would say "*C'est la vie*," meaning "That's life," although we are in Adelaide, in the southern hemisphere. As I breathed in the freshness of the sea breeze with the wind blowing into my face while my feet dug into the fine sand as I strolled along Gleneagh Beach, I pondered the different lives of the people on different areas of the planet we live in. Here, I see the Aussies taking their dogs for their morning stroll, all different kinds of pedigree I have not seen before. In quite a similar situation, a few years ago on a visit to Jerusalem, it was another strange sight for me to see so many Jews in their traditional hats on the Sabbath. I often wondered what other people's lives were like, and even your best friend's, life may not be quite like your life, as in the different lives of these people that I know.

My cousin Nor is a fun, interesting, helpful, and attractive girl with a heart of gold. We grew up together and there is much affection between us as she, born an Aries while I a Sagittarian, belong to the same fire signs of the horoscope and we both enjoyed similar hobbies. Although she is one and a half years younger than me, she is more hyperactive and had lived abroad in the Western world from an early age. She was the one to teach me about the finer things in life, and between us we shared many friends. As we saw a lot of each other in between her home breaks due to her father's career in the foreign service, we partied a lot, went swimming at beaches and public swimming pools, and shared adult stories at bedtime together. With Nor, life was never boring because she made life interesting and her funny ways used to send giggles through my spine. Whenever she was abroad, we would write letters to each other, exchanging stories of our grown-up lives. From a gawky child, her years abroad had polished her image and she grew up to be an attractive teenager with the gift of gab and mannerisms enough to tantalize many admirers. Her worldly air that she carried herself with is only the image she wanted people to see, but once you get to know her, she is the most sincere person you will ever know.

At six years old, Nor left our house where she stayed for one year to join her parents in Canberra, where her father was serving his first posting as the assistant high commissioner of Malaya. She enjoyed her childhood days in Canberra as she recalled mixing with the Aussie children from her kindergarten school and eating fresh fish and chips that her mother cooked. Nor's mom was a good cook and she loved tending to her vegetable garden in Canberra. She also remembered going to outdoor cinemas with her mother with great excitement and to the farmer's Cut house for crayfish. She remembered her wonderful neighbors Uncle Cyril and Aunty Mary who had two children, Andrew and Elizabeth, whom she befriended and played with in their tree house. Mommy was always learning new dishes to cook from Aunty Mary. In Autumn the leaves would turn into a magnificent color of yellow and red in front of the parliament house. She would dig up the worms and go fishing with Daddy. The seaside of Kalbarri was a place they visited regularly, slurping oysters that grew on the rocks. She had wonderful memories of Canberra surrounded by family and her friendly Australian neighbors and friends.

When she was eight years old, she went to America with her parents as her father was asked to resume his duties in Washington, DC. On the way they stopped in London for three days, where she enjoyed the bustling city with red double-decker buses.

In Washington, DC, they lived at Linnean Avenue and later moved to a beautiful house near Rock Creek Park and she attended the Ben Murch Elementary School, where Nor met and mixed freely with the American Jewish children. Every morning she would walk to school with her two younger brothers Nordin and Sydney, carrying with her packed sardine or tuna sandwiches prepared by Mommy. On the way to school, Nor noticed many children selling jellied apples decorated with honey and nuts on a red wagon. Nor and her brothers managed to get one of the wagons and started to sell honeyed apples too and spent the money they earned on their favorite food. Every Saturday, Daddy would send them to study at the Islamic center to learn Arabic. Nor still remembered the day when Daddy forgot to fetch her two younger brothers from the Islamic center and had Mommy frantic with worry. When Daddy eventually found the two boys, they were on the other side of town at their old house at Linnean Avenue. One of her best memories of her childhood in America was when every year the children from the different embassies were invited to the White House and were entertained by clowns. Nor managed to catch a glimpse of the First Lady. Meanwhile, back at the Malaysian Embassy, Mommy had the basement transformed into a lovely big hall where the children held concerts and fashion shows. Nor and her elder sister Yam would be dressed in pretty frocks sewn by their talented Mommy and always a duplicate of each other.

Mommy was very creative and observant and would cook three hundred Malaysian dishes all on her own until the wee hours in the morning, depending only on her black coffee and cigarettes to keep her awake. Nor and her sister would help with the flower arrangement while she did the food and fruit carving, an art learned from her Thai helpers. Every weekend they would have family outings with the rest of the embassy families and went camping or have picnics in the woods at different places in summer. One memorable summer was when the whole family drove up to the Canadian hills, stopping at the Niagara Falls and camping up in the hills and passing through the wonderful scenery from America right up to Canada. It was her best holiday as a child.

The Malaysian High Commission of Malaya was first set up in Washington, DC. While her father was serving as the acting high commissioner of Malaya, Nor and Yam participated in many events to promote Malaya. Every Merdeka Day, which is the National Day of Malaya, the embassy would host the foreign dignitaries with champagne and toast. The children would be involved too and Nor and Yam would be asked by Mommy to perform a song and dance called *Bunga Melor*, or Flowers of Malaysia, a popular Malay song in the fifties about the fragrant melur flower. Nor and Yam would be dressed in a traditional outfit, the *kebaya*, sewn by Mommy. The Embassy would also host tea parties for women's organization and promote Malayan films.

After her father's posting to America, they were posted to Bangkok, where Daddy was appointed as the dean of the diplomatic corps. Mommy's creativity led her to learn to sew and make slippers and purses with sequins sewn on for evening wear, and the leftover brocade fabric would be used to make dresses for Nor's doll collection. Daddy and Mommy would host many functions, the most tedious being the formal black-tie dinners, where attention was given to every detail. Mommy, being very observant, having observed many black-tie dinners held at her mother and stepfather's house when she was a young girl, displayed her talent for entertaining in style. She would start the evening with a chicken soup and end the evening with a pumpkin pudding Asian style, a menu adopted and perfected on her later posting to Moscow. Nor was also very well versed in the art of entertaining, trained by her parents, and had a flair for style. She would set the table for the black-tie dinners, decorated with lotus flowers napkins and name cards with the proper titles on a small silver tray.

The title of "His Excellency" would be used for the ambassador on the name card and also in conversations addressing him. Next to the ambassador would be seated two ladies. After dinner, the men would be led to a separate room for coffee with cognac and cigars where they would discuss politics and play billiards. The ladies would adjourn to another room where they would have coffee and biscuits. The dinner would be finished by 11:00 p.m. always. Nor was put in charge of the embassy liquor store. She and her father would sit down together to take stock of all the wine cases, liquor, champagne, vodka, and the expensive Dom Pérignon. That was how she educated herself on the different kinds of wine and their origin and years produced, from the cheaper to the more expensive wines.

Nor's recollection of her father was that although he was a doting family man in some ways, like taking them to family holidays and outings, he could also be very stern and strict and was difficult to persuade. When Nor was young and wanted to go out with her other friends outside the embassy, she would ask for his permission to go out. If the answer was "No" or silence, even if Nor continued to try and persuade him until she fell asleep next to him waiting for his answer, it would still be "No." He would only allow her to go out with children of the embassy staff of Malaysia or from other foreign embassies. Once in Bangkok, Daddy asked her one day if Nor had any plans for the evening, and Nor retorted in exasperation that she was not doing anything as he wouldn't allow her to go out with her school friends. Her father asked if she could show around the teenage son of the Canadian Prime Minister who was on a visit to Bangkok with him. It was her first date alone with a boy Nor recalled, and they went to the exclusive club called Caesar's Palace for dinner. In order to appear grown up and sophisticated, Nor ordered Coke with vodka, called a black Russian, and ended up vomiting as she was showing her foreign guest around Bangkok by night. While she was growing up as a teenager in Bangkok, she met many foreign journalists from many like The Associated Press and foreign boys from different embassies from her school and through friends, among whom were a Spanish guy called Carlos and a Swedish guy called David, whom she dated. She also became good friends with a member of the "Malakul" family called Tuptim, whom she is still in touch with till today and exchanges news of their families with them. Tuptim's daughter became an actress in Hollywood, and in the beginning of her career Tuptim followed her daughter all over the globe. Being young and an attractive teenager and full of life, Nor could be mischievous too and on one occasion hosted a party at her residence while her parents were on holiday. She invited one hundred of her friends and classmates, complete with a band. The noise received the attention of the acting ambassador, who called her the next day and queried if her parents knew about the party she hosted. She replied, out of fear, that she got permission from her parents, although that was not the case, and lucky for her the incident was not mentioned again. She got away with the little white lie to protect herself. Nor also played host to her school friends by inviting them to lunch at the embassy during lunch breaks and being chauffeured back to school again after their lunch. She was also well versed in the art of entertaining and could not wait to display the art that she acquired from her mother. During their stay in Bangkok, her father spent a lot of time on the golf course and her mother spent time playing bridge and mahjong, and she was left with a lot of time on her hands, spending most of her time at the swimming pool with her school friends while her elder sister had started dating.

After Bangkok, Nor's father was sent to Russia as the ambassador with a three-month break on home leave in Kuala Lumpur, where she met her cousins and relatives and partied with them. After Bangkok, life in Russia, it being a Communist country, was very different. No one was allowed to travel more than fifty kilometers outside of Moscow even for hobbies like fishing and hunting or for saunas, without prior permission. The winters were cold and bleak. Thank God for the diplomatic stores where she could get some necessities. In those diplomatic stores, mainly crystals were plentiful at an unimaginable price of USD 2 for a crystal bowl, and became the favorite haunt of the embassy staff, who had nowhere else to shop. They would frequently go to Helsinki in order to get toilet paper, salads at the market, and clothes. Nor's father was also the ambassador accredited to Mongolia, Poland, Hungary, Czechoslovakia, Romania, Bulgaria, and all the Eastern Bloc countries, which Daddy would visit every few months, taking his family with him. Once they went on the Trans-Siberian railway, which is famed for its beautiful and plush interior with red velvet curtains and crisp cotton bed linens. Nor loved the antique brass door handles and the expensive silverware used in the restaurant wagon where the butler served caviar, salmon, and chicken kiev. Most of all, Nor loved the sound of the engine as the train moved along the route from Moscow to Siberia to Irkutsk and Ulan Bator. It was an experience of a lifetime that Daddy wanted his family to have, Nor said.

Another highlight of Nor's stay in Moscow, she said, was when Daddy was conferred the Tan Sri, which was the highest medal given to government officers for their service by the Malaysian government. Daddy, as usual, thought instead of wasting the government's money to go back to Malaysia to receive the award it would be better for the prime minister of Malaysia to visit Moscow, which he did and was received in typical Malaysian hospitality by the embassy staff. There was a small and private ceremony in which the Prime Minister presented Daddy the title "Tan Sri".

In order to spice up her teenage life in Moscow, Nor mixed with the other foreigners from other embassies and foreign journalists from *Le Monde* and *Daily Express* and from other countries. Nor began dating Peter, who was a young Australian diplomat of Hungarian descent and who also became a favorite of her parents as Peter played cards, especially gin rummy, with them. Peter would host regular parties at his apartment while serving caviar and champagne. Peter was a polished host and would serve his favorite Armagnac, which was a cognac from a province in France. There were no nightclubs in Moscow at that time and the embassies were permitted to have their own clubs. It was during one of these outings in the bitterly cold winter that Peter remembered very well because Nor was wearing "hot pants" above her stockings, which Mommy, who loved seeing Nor in the latest fashion, had brought back from Helsinki on her recent trip. It was also at that time that Peter and his friend Antonio, whom Nor had just met, were fighting for Nor's attention.

Russia's population was categorized from a young age as to their ability and usefulness to the government. For instance, ballerinas were considered as people who did good for the country and they were given a better standard of living as opposed to other normal professions. The KGB officers were given a higher standard of living and has access to imported goods and *dachas*, or villas, in the countryside. Although all embassies employed Russians as maids and drivers, it was not often they were invited to the homes of Russians except for certain reasons. On one occasion, a friend of Nora and his wife, who were working with the Volvo car company, were invited to bid for a painting of Wassily Kandinsky, a famous Russian painter. Bids started at only USD300 when it could fetch millions now.

Nor managed to acquire a fish porcelain Heissen set for USD100 from a Russian family leaving for America. A Jewish painter who was leaving for America was commissioned by Daddy to paint Nor every day for a month. Nor was able to indulge in her hobby of collecting various precious ornaments seized during the Russian Revolution, such as samovars and antique silver boxes. Nor learned to speak Russian through her Russian tutors and was able to converse with the non-English-speaking Russians. This made her life easier in many ways and enabled her to mix with the mixed community and Russians and especially to find her way around Moscow. One of the advantages of being able to speak Russian was that it enabled her to converse with Antonio, a young Italian guy and a friend of Peter who could not converse in English but was fluent in Russian. They conversed in Russian, and this communication led to their marriage later on. Antonio was working at the Fiat car company in Moscow and lived in the Leninsky Prospekt, which was a nice green area where most foreigners lived, including some of the Malaysian Embassy staff.

It was during her teenage years as a society debutante among the diplomatic circle that she met Antonio and decided that he, among all other suitors, would be the man in her life. Their first meeting happened when Nor went with her regular escort Peter to a party and met Antonio for the first time. He looked dashing in his safari suit and came with his friend Franco. Having confided in her mother about Antonio, Mommy asked Nor to invite Antonio to dinner at the embassy after having approved of his good looks and thick black hair and blue eyes that changed color, Mommy remarked. Nor invited Antonio for dinner and to meet Daddy, who refused to come down to dinner despite numerous calls from Nor's younger sister to bring him down. He eventually did at midnight. Meanwhile, Antonio was sweating heavily in his nervousness at meeting Nor's dad, who hardly spoke a word nor replied when Antonio told him that he was asking for Nor's hand in marriage. Nor's mother, taken in by Antonio's charm and eager to host another big event, started making wedding preparations and wrote to her family back home to order the hand-woven silk material interwoven with gold thread called "songket," which was the usual wedding fabric for couples in Malaysia. Nor and Antonio themselves reupholstered the wedding chair for the dais and covered it in green *songket* from Trengganu, a state famous for *songket* weaving. The wedding was done in a typically Malay style with three hundred guests and Antonio's family, who came from Italy and stayed in Moscow for a month with the newly wedded couple.

Life in Russia might have been difficult for their own people during those times in the sixties and seventies, but for the diplomatic circle it was a privileged and interesting life of diplomats, foreign journalists, local artists and painters, and visiting celebrities. Because it was a small, tightly knit society, if one was in the circle it was easy to mingle among the people there. Antonio managed to meet Sean Connery, the famous Hollywood actor, at a hotel and invited him to his house for an Italian dinner. Sean Connery liked Antonio because he was the only one who did not call him "James Bond." On another occasion, the British singer Cliff Richard came to Moscow and Nor was asked by her friend to cook an Italian meal at her friend's house for Cliff. Cliff Richard was very nice, Nor recalled, and she made him sing "Summer Holidays." The next day, he invited Nor and her friend to lunch at the well-known National Hotel. Nor and Antonio remained in Moscow even after Nor's parents left permanently for Malaysia. Antonio worked with Fiat until the 1970's, and Nor followed Antonio back to Italy, where she remained for the next twenty years of her life.

Nor's home in Italy was at Parma, and not far away was where the famous clothes designer Giorgio Armani was born. Piacenza is the home of musicians and where the national anthem of Italy was composed by Verdi. Antonio's family lived in this same little town of one hundred thousand people where everyone knew and cared for each other. According to Nor, they could be mistaken for intrusive people, not because they were being nosey but because they cared about you. For instance, if Nora should come back late at night, the neighbours would ask her why, and if the children fell or got sick the whole town would know. If anyone was buying a dishwasher, which was considered a luxury item rather than necessity in those days, it would be discussed within the family at the table during Sunday lunch before a purchase was made. At mealtimes in an Italian house, everything would be discussed during the five-course meals, from politics to everything at all to do with the family. Everyone knew Nor and would hug her on the street whenever they met her. Such was their friendliness toward one another in the neighborhood.

The Italians, according to Nora, showed love in a different way: by telling you what to do. This was because they were concerned about you and cared for you. It was something she learned to understand after years of living among them and was no longer irritated by it. Nor admitted that it was not easy in the beginning to live with Antonio's family because of the language barrier and the difference in religion. Being devout Catholics, Antonio's mother at first had a grudge against Nor for being the reason her son converted to Islam. Antonio's younger sister married a priest after he left the priesthood. The former priest died early and she remarried another Italian man, whose main preoccupation was reading, and they later moved to Rome. Antonio worked as an engineer and supported his younger brother throughout his days in university. Nor said that she learned about her religion through living in another country and by reading books about religion. When she refused to eat pork as it was forbidden in Islam, her Italian friends could not understand how she could refuse such a delicious meat.

When her daughter Anastasia first started fasting at ten years old, her teacher approached Nor, concerned that Anastasia was not getting enough food in her growing years. Her mother-in-law was very religious and always carried her rosary beads around with her in her hand, quite similar to the Muslim prayer beads called *tasbih*. Both being women of strong personalities, they did not take to each other in the beginning. Her mother-in-law, Rose, still wanted to choose underpants for her son, being a possessive mother, while Nor was trying her best to show her mother-in-law that she was a capable and an efficient wife. It was only after Karim, her third child, was born that Rose relented, and later, when Nor moved to Malaysia with Antonio, she confessed to her daughter-in-law over the telephone that she loved her like her own daughter.

To quote Nor's own words when referring to her parents-in-law and Antonio's family. "Bless their souls as they are no longer around but the Sunday lunches with them gave my children much joy and pleasure with their Italian cousins, aunts and uncles and the warmth of the Italians till this day touches my heart."

The Italians would take great pains to look nice and be well dressed, with matching shoes and handbags, as it is their pride and joy to look good. They look forward to the different seasons when they could change their clothes as well as their plants as they are very house proud. Every summer they would rush out to buy potted plants and Nor would follow suit and plant different herbs on her balcony. She would sit out on the balcony in summer while doing her crocheting and knitting or take Anastasia to the parks. The government schools were very good and the teachers dedicated and concerned about the children. Sometimes, Anastasia would push her little sister

Miriam in a pram, and as they passed the women on the street they would say to her, "Oh what a beautiful baby but you are more beautiful," in order not to hurt her feelings and young ego. The Italians loved children, and this amazing little town was a lovely place to raise children in. Everyone knew Nora and Anastasia in Piacenza as Anastasia was often seen cycling in the village with her little sister. Earlier, when Nora was expecting her second child Miriam and a third one later, she could not go up and down the stairs and the bread man and the milkman would voluntarily climb upstairs to her apartment to deliver her daily bread and milk. Nora also learned where to get fresh eggs from chickens and how to bottle tomatoes cook Italian food from her father-in-law, who was a good cook. Her father-in-law doted on her and they would sometimes have coffee and a chitchat. Nor's relationship with her mother-in-law improved as time went by when Nora helped her with her housework on the maid's off days. Life was so blissful in Parma that Nor decided to stay back while Antonio went to Tashkent to set up a factory with his partner. Nor liked her life at Piacenza as she was able to have a closely knitted family and enjoyed their closeness. Once when she and Antonio were going out to dinner, his grandmother asked caringly if there was not enough food in the house to eat. The older generation never went out to eat like the new generation did. Antonio was a workaholic and used to leave for work even before the children left for school. Nor would visit her hairdresser at 6:00 a.m., then go back and prepare breakfast for the children.

In Nor's own words as she related the events of her life :

"After eight years in the USSR, Moscow, we decided to move to Italy and start a new life. Antonio left the FIAT company and decided to venture into business with his uncle who then lived in Reggio Emilia in Italy, a region famous for its gastronomy. Parma, although a province, is noted for its Parmesan cheese and Parma ham. We were therefore living in an agricultural zone, surrounded by farms. My life in Italy revolved around my husband and his family. Without any children at that time, I was free to do as I pleased, learnt the language, the culture and its people. Going back home yearly gave me much courage to go back and confront my own demons The countryside was too peaceful for my liking but as I had so much time on my hands, I took the courage to make friends and interact with others. That went well as I learnt so many wonderful things from the Italian women who are extremely gifted. I learned how to crochet, knit, bottle my pickled vegetables and tomatoes in late summer for the cold winter ahead. Life was too busy as Italian women are spic and span, extremely house proud and had beautiful clean homes. One could sleep even in the kitchen as it was immaculately clean. After my first child, life changed dramatically. Never had I imagine that we had to dedicate so much time, effort, love and patience to this first child we had. We moved to Piacenza but as days, months and years went by, things got easier and it became a part of our daily lives as 'breathing.'

"Through the years we liked the idea of having children and we did have another two later on. Sunday lunches were a must at grandparents' house where we would sit for hours going from course to course. We would be lucky if we finished by 3:00 p.m. It was those lovely Sundays where my children would meet their aunts and uncles and cousins. We would all pitch in and do our respective chores to make the day eventful. I love and cherish those days as the children were growing and we had

wonderful experiences and memories that
linger on till this very day. Life in the country
was conducive to children growing up. We
had our own bicycles and almost every other
day, we would be cycling away. The small
town of Caorso where I lived was perfect as
we knew everybody and everybody knew us.
The butcher, the baker were all our friends
and such compassionate people and ever so
caring. Without doubt, I learnt a lot from the
Italians till the day I die. Missing my family
back home was always a part of my life all
those years. Fortunately, we were always able to
come home to Malaysia for the three months
of summer school holidays. In Italy, in summer,
most times we would go to the seaside in the
day and sleep in the mountains when night fell.
The pediatricians in Italy always recommended
taking the children to the seaside in summer as
the air is good for the health, as it would prevent
them from catching the dreadful 'flu' in winters.
A month or so camping in the mountains or
being at the seaside was a yearly affair. The rest
of the summer, I would take my children home
to my parents which they would then spend

time with their Malaysian grandparents whom they were fond of, and their Malaysian and Thai-American cousins and I would catch up on the lost time with my Malaysian cousins as well. At my late parents' home, there would be warm bondage between all of us. Those were moments which my children and I cherish again till now. Life in Italy was never dull, on the contrary, as it was complete with me rather busy being a mother and housekeeper, but fulfilling to say the least. As my late mother fell ill, I also thought it was time to go back with the children to home where my roots were. Home, where I felt all the comfort I could imagine. Antonio, being a workaholic, had decided to venture into a new country called Uzbekistan. I therefore gave him my blessings and off he went to venture and explore the possibility, while my children and I packed a small container of personal belongings with me and moved to Kuala Lumpur.

"I may have disappointed my in-laws by wanting to leave Italy as they were my family too but I did want my children to know of Malaysian life and culture as I wanted to expose them to the Asian way of life, which is totally different from the Italian. My desire was for them to be introduced to both and they can easily choose later on in life where they would want to stay. We struggled the first few years, the climate, the food, the language and many other things that we missed in Italy which we could not find in Malaysia. I really am not sure whether or not, I did the right thing but what's done is done and I can only look back and say, 'It's been quite a ride.' Life is like a merry-go-round because it has its ups and downs. But our experiences in life is what teaches us to grow.

The situation in Tashkent was not suitable for children as there were no international schools her children could attend. Although Uzbekistan was a Muslim country, Islam was not really practiced except for a segment of fundamentalists. It was quite a backward place then and known only as an agricultural country where all sorts of melons were grown as a livelihood. It was also a difficult time for Nor because her beloved mother was bedridden with diabetes and was hospitalized for many months. Sometime ago, before she had Anastasia, she had gone to Europe and Switzerland with her parents to accompany her father on a working holiday. While shopping, her mother had suffered a stroke and had not really recovered since then.

With her elder sister away in America tending to the family business and her two brothers also working overseas, Nor felt responsible for her ailing mother even though she did make regular visits home. With Antonio in Tashkent, she made up her mind to take her children back to Malaysia. She was also concerned about the children's schooling since English language was not taught in schools in Tashkent. She also worried about the children's religion as they grew up. She found an apartment near her parents' residence so she could visit them and enroll her children in the International School nearby. Antonio came back to visit them regularly whenever he could get himself away from his business. He was hopeful that he could sell his factory in the near future to join Nor. Her mother's illness took a long time and she never quite recovered fully. She eventually passed away, leaving Nor's father, who was devoted to her late mother, in the big house alone. With her mother, gone Nor found it difficult to leave her father alone and her children were happy in the international school. They mixed well with the Malaysian children and enjoyed getting to know their Malaysian and Thai cousins whenever they came back for holidays.

Italy seemed a long way now, although her mother-in-law and Antonio's family frequently telephoned her as they missed the Malaysian girl who was a popular figure in the town of Parma. Nor felt that her home was now in Malaysia and she enjoyed being with her family and relatives where she grew up. So she decided to go back to her roots. Nor had never been one to dwell on material possessions as she had always been a warm and caring person who would put aside her needs in order to help another person. In this case, she felt her parents needed her most then. She loved cooking Italian food for her children and husband whenever he visited Malaysia, and her friends, who enjoyed her Italian culinary expertise, especially her roast duck and date pudding. Although she spoke regularly of her house and collection of antiquities that she left behind and missed and hope that one day she would be able to bring them back to Malaysia.

After half a lifetime of globetrotting Nor had chosen to return to the land where she was born and grew up in the early years of her life. The country where she had fond memories of the people and the happy times she spent before she ventured out to foreign lands. Although her teenage life was spent mainly in Thailand where she has kept in touch till today with her old school friends. Some of them have achieved good positions in their professions in different countries and Nor rejoiced in their glory as Nor had always been generous in her feelings for others. Her children too shared her love for her motherland until it was time for them to leave Malaysia in order to pursue their own careers. Her eldest child, Anastasia left for Wales to study law and ended working as a solicitor in Cardiff. Her longtime boyfriend, Gareth, whom she met while studying in the International School in Kuala Lumpur, moved back to England after his father had completed his services in Malaysia. While Gareth practised as a barrister, Anastasia worked as a solicitor with the refugees mainly from Iran and eastern Europe, helping them to seek asylum in the United Kingdom. Together, they are saving enough money to buy a little townhouse in Rugby, in the English countryside and planning their future together after a long friendship since schooldays. Nor's second daughter, Miriam, who inherited her mother's culinary talent, completed her university in Barcelona but decided to start her own business in Bristol so as to reunite with her elder sister in the UK. Acting on her own initiative, she approached the Council of Bristol to convert the vacant land in the centre of Bristol into a family entertainment park. This premise used to be the favourite haunt of drug addicts and alchoholics and became their refuge. She and her business partner, an English girl, started by buying a small container and transformed it into a little coffee shop. Another friend of Miriam, bought a double decker bus and turned it into a Mexican cafetaria next to hers. In her little container-cafe, Miriam prepared her own organic cuisine derived from Italian recipes which became very popular that her business took off by leaps and bounds, that she is now doing catering for almost a thousand people. Not a bad start for a young and inexperienced girl from Italy who started only with her "guts" to start her career in a foreign land. She has been approached by many young entrepreneurs to expand her business which she is considering while at the same time, she has not forgotten her commitment to the Bristol community by involving herself in the social and welfare of the people. Nor's youngest son, Karim has decided to join his sisters abroad having spent most of his life in Malaysia since he was seven years old. Nor, upon reflection on her own life, understands the need to be away and travel around the globe as she had been in her youth, although she hopes that one day they will choose to return to Malaysia.

"Sunflower weary of time
Who countest the steps of the sun,
Seeking after the sweet golden clime
When the traveller's journey is done"

Piacenza Italy

Antonnio with Miriam

Nor and Antonnio

Nor and family in UK

Nor and Miriam at cafe

Nor in Piacenza

Nor with Anastasia and Miriam

Chapter 4

THE MISSIONARIES

(a) "Mother Theresa" of Melbourne

"I Slept and Dreamt That Life Was A Beauty, I
Woke Up To Find That Life Was a Duty"

—Anonymous

Melbourne, being a cosmopolitan city of four million
people may appear safe and quiet to visitors.

With the influx of the migrant population, the city
has become divided into different communities inhabited
by individual races. Gangland fights are becoming frequent
incidences in Little Italy or suburbs where mostly the Lebanese
reside. A few years ago, the notorious Lebanon drug criminal
Tony Mokbel or Fat Tony was finally put behind bars after
years of investigation by the Melbourne police. He had started

Melbourne's drug trade with his brothers, and for decades had ruled the suburbs and drug-laden streets of Sydney Road and Lygon Street.

The areas of South Caulfield, St. Kilda, Armadale, Brunswick, Sunshine, Brighton, Coburg, Port Melbourne, South Yarra, Essendon, Richmond, and Lygon Street were not spared as they became the regular haunts or residences of the drug kings, and killings and gunshots could happen anywhere. No one area was spared; likewise, the drug kings have become sophisticated people with excellent manners and old-fashioned but respectable designer clothes, having come a long way from their humble beginnings.

The life story of Tony Mokbel who is still held in prison in Australia since his capture is amazing. After a luxurious life as a drug lord, he was on the run from shelter to shelter, living in barns on the farm land of his sympathetic relatives and finally escaping on a barge to a Greek island. There he lived a short lived comfortable life, incognito, with his long time mistress and child only to be arrested in a restaurant by his long time pursuer of twenty years. He was put behind bars in Melbourne prison. His long time mistress, wanting to start a new life for herself and her daughter left him for another man.

In 2002, Melbourne drug wars escalated with the inclusion of another notorious figure of Lebanese descent, Mokbel, who was on the hunt for at least a decade when the body count began to mount, sometimes for personal or sometimes business reason. A veteran crime reporter, John Silvester, who thought there were simply too many people in Melbourne trying to deal in drugs, saw it as a game of musical chairs in which the loser was usually shot.

Since the eighties Melbourne had been associated with criminal gangs and warlords. The city was in the grip of if not a crime wave, then at least hooliganism with the Hoddle Street Lairies, including the notorious brothers John and Edward Peddy, taking over hotels and raiding bakeries where they could eat for free. In 1892, there was an alarming if temporary increase in domestic burglaries in both the city and suburbs of Melbourne, with thieves entering houses by the front window and leisurely proceeding to search various rooms for valuables. They would turn up the gas in the drawing room, eat cake, help themselves to wine, and entertain themselves with card games. By the mid-1890s a series of private bills were brought before the New South Wales parliament designed to curb prostitution and larrikinism and to allow burglars to be flogged in. In 1903, a third son of an Irish immigrant called John Wren founded the illegal City Tattersall Club, having been involved with big wins on horses during the races such as the Melbourne Cup. For years he conducted a successful period with the police and authorities and used his big earnings to nurse his neighborhood and donate to the Catholic Church and the needy. The notorious areas of Sydney Road, Fitzroy, and Collingwood became their regular haunts and his gaming business made him a millionaire many times over even though there was a smell of corruption about him. Other famous names like Melbourne's Leslie "Squizzy Taylor," sometimes known as the Turk—a self-promoter, murderer, pimp, and grass supplier who came from the beautiful coastal village of Brighton—received uncalled for admiration from the wrong side of the public and became the biggest preoccupation of Sgt. David O'Donnell in Nicholson Street in Fitzroy, a hippy community. O'Donell became the most powerful crime fighter for the next thirty years in Melbourne.

The rolling hills of the Yarra Valley and the Dandenongs may appear quiet and deceptive as they lie in the quietness of the suburbs, but this was a notorious gangland, operating in the city and neighboring vicinity, and kept Melbourne's police squad pretty busy for decades. It is not surprising, what with Australia's early history as the settlement of convicts and the later influx of refugees, particularly in Melbourne and Sydney. This gave rise to gangsterism, prostitution, and drug dealing, among other crimes, among the varied communities. The police squad and authorities try hard to control the gangland activities through social welfare services involving public awareness, and this is how a community social worker from Malaysia, Nora, came into the picture after moving to Sydney from her homeland.

I first met Nora when I was introduced to her by a friend when I needed transport to go to the airport to catch my flight back to Kuala Lumpur. Through Nora I got to know other Malaysians and Muslims living around her area in Werribbee, and apparently there is a big community of 1,000 students and 2,000 other Malaysians who have resided here by virtue of their marriage to Australians, not to mention the non-Muslim Malaysians who have migrated to Melbourne. Nora's work as a social worker revolved mainly around her community, where I have met families like Maryati from Sulawesi, a Lebanese lady called Wati, who is ever so helpful, and another Middle Eastern-Thai family with three beautiful daughters, Hafiza, Nafisah, and Sara. The girls were the product of their mother's second marriage to a Middle Eastern Muslim man, who died of a heart attack. The family was living on social security as their mother was suffering from arthritis and unable to work. Nora, being the magnanimous person that she is, adopted the girls as sisters to her only daughter, Zowie, who became their godsister, spoiling them with her monthly wages from work.

Nora lives in a large single-story house with her husband John and John's mother, who at eighty-eight is an avid facebook user and has many friends all over the world. She is bedridden as she suffers from diabetes. Nora's eldest son, Jacob, works as a journalist and photographer in Afghanistan and followed the footsteps of her mother. Nora's house is an open house as she has and would welcome anyone in need of a home. She has had countless foster children of different nationalities, some of whom are Australians, in the course of her work as a community worker. Just two years ago, she adopted two Malaysian girls, Dewi, twelve years old, and her sister Dani, who together with their brother were sent through an illegal syndicate from Malaysia to work as child laborers on a farm in Melbourne. Their mother had remarried an Indonesian man. Dewi and her sister lived on the farm together with other workers, separated from their brother, and Dewi was impregnated by one of the Indonesian workers. Dewi and her sister Dani tried to run away and that was how they came under Nora's care. Nora, upon knowing her plight, adopted Dewi, now fourteen years old, to deliver her daughter, whom she named Sara. Now Dewi works in a retail shop and is taking a hospitality course at the same time. Her daughter, who was born with brain damage, had to undergo brain surgery when she was just a year old but recovered well and is now the most intelligent and talkative girl her age. Dewi's sister Dani fell in love with an Australian boy, who after initially refusing to adopt Islam as his religion, finally relented and agreed to become a Muslim in order to marry Dani. They have now moved to Queensland to get a new job. Dewi and Dani's story has a happy ending, even though this is not always the case for many other refugees that we have come to hear of from Nora's experiences.

Norasiah Hassan Simkin

Nora originally came from Selangor where she received her secondary education at the Methodist girls' school. They lived at Bukit Travers where her father was attached to the police force. She started work as a teacher in Sandakan, where her students were older than her and it caused some complications when the older boys tried to be "fresh" with her up, to a point where one of them used black magic in order to entice her. Because of the unpleasant working conditions, she left her job to follow her father to Penang. While in Penang, she involved herself in voluntary social work as she noticed that Malaysia in 1976 did not have a welfare system, and social work was run by the nuns who were not compassionate to the plight of single mothers and juvenile prostitutes. She was very keen to fight for social justice and sympathized with the victims of our society. In her involvement with the reform school of Mr. Poh Liong Kok, which was a halfway home for those youngsters, she met the girlfriend of Malaysia's notorious gangster Botak Chin and others. She wanted to introduce an education system like physical education, craft, and English language. She disliked the way the center was run and the mistreatment of prisoners and thereby needed money to cover expenses for the center.

Being young and compassionate, she became a bit of a rolling stone when the situation did not suit her temperament. When she saw an advertisement in the newspaper for a job as an operational clerk at the Air Express International at Bayan Lepas Airport, she applied for it. When she came for the interview, the manager, Mr. Siva, tried to dissuade her from the job as it was lowly paid—RM180 plus an allowance of RM50 for petrol— and told her that it was a man's job. Nora, being the confident and outspoken girl that she was, reiterated that it was not mentioned in the advertisement that the position was for a male, and that if she was given three months to try out the job she could prove that she was just as capable as any other man. If she could not prove herself capable within the given three months, the manager could sack her or vice versa, she implored. Nora proved herself well as she was able to handle customers because of her good personal relationship with them and her negotiation skills. After three months her salary was reviewed and she was paid RM230 plus petrol allowance and stayed for three years.

It was while Nora was working at Air Express International that she met John at the Flying Club nearby. John was looking for a drink and Nora bought him a bottle of water. John was working then as a technician in the Royal Australian Air Force and was stationed in Penang. The next thing she knew, John asked her if she could help find accommodation for his mother, who was visiting him in Penang. Nora was a bit agitated by this foreigner who only after meeting her once was asking for another favor, but she managed to get his mother a room at Wisma Putra's lodging. Their friendship blossomed and one day John proposed to Nora, who told him that first he had to meet her father as it was quite rare in those days to marry whites or *mat sallehs*. Nora's father, although sorry at the thought of probably having to lose her favorite daughter, only questioned John if he was a patient man, because his daughter was an overconfident and self-centered girl at that age and needed a very patient man who could handle her. The fact that he was Australian did not bother Nora's father because John was already a Muslim convert before he approached Nora's dad. They got married at the RAAF base according to rituals and also at the mosque. John had earlier been a Buddhist follower and had adopted the Buddhist way of life, which was to do good in life, as often preached by their leaders Confucius and his followers. However, he realized that there's a missing element to connect oneself to him and the missing element was Allah, the Almighty, and that was how he came to accept Islam as his religion.

Nora later enrolled herself in an air freight training course organized by Singapore Airlines and decided to fly to Singapore on Singapore Airlines rather than Malaysian Airlines, which she had earlier booked. That saved her life because the flight MH10 was hijacked in Johore and her relatives sympathized with her, not knowing that her last-minute decision changed her fate and kept her alive for her next venture into a foreign country with John. After the MH10 incident, John was recalled back to Australia to serve at the RAAF base in Laverton, Australia, where their eldest son Jacob was born. While there, Nora took the opportunity to form a childcare group for wives and mothers to get together to support one another. In those days, the Asian wives of the Australian army or navy officers were being frowned upon and scrutinized as they were among the few and were referred to as "tiger bar girls." Once Nora overheard a conversation between two Australian ladies who referred to the Asian wives as ladies of the "trap bar." The conversation enraged Nora and she retaliated by correcting them that Asian ladies made good bed companions and good wives and that was a good enough reason for Australian men to marry them. In general, in those days even the air force men looked down on Thai women as they could not converse in English and used pidgin when conversing in English. So generally the migrants in Australia were not all accepted and were being scrutinized.

The support group helped in easing the feeling of homesickness among the Asian wives who missed home but were able to meet other Asian wives residing in Australia. They also organized English classes for the wives from Thailand, especially those who could not speak English. They also helped to set up two *halal* meat shops for the Muslims in the Preston area and nearby.

In Melbourne there was already a Malay village near Sydney Road where Malaysian students from nearby areas like Coburg and Broadmeadows congregate. Apart from the students there were also the Muslims who had chosen to reside in Melbourne as permanent residents. They also introduced physical exercise and sports like netball for the RAAF ladies, as well as flying doctors and cinemas. Later John was transferred to the Sydney RAAF base for five years and Nora again involved herself in the ladies' support group where many more facilities were available, like a swimming pool. Just before John retired from the RAAF, they moved to Melbourne, where Nora opened a café called Café Noor at Footscray for five years. Here, at Footscray, which is the Vietnamese area of Melbourne, she met many homeless youths whom she became guardian to. John's work with the RAAF took him away often and Nora was free to indulge in her social work as well as running the café. There were a lot of street kids whose parents were single mothers hooked on alcohol and gambling. The runaway children would be sleeping at the railway stations, having nowhere to go and no food to eat. The system then was the Australian government body, which is called center link or social security, only helped children after sixteen years of age. Before sixteen, the children would be under the care of their parents or parent. There was a case of a single mother who herself was an alcoholic and a drug user. Her twelve-year-old son used to go to Nora's shop to find food. Apparently, he'd been on the street for two years, sleeping at railway stations. Once he hitched a ride from a truck driver and was given beer and cigarettes and was afterward raped. Nora felt sorry for the boy and adopted him into her home. Afterward there were countless street kids adopted by Nora into her own home after John retired. This inspired Nora to get a diploma of welfare studies at the Preston TAFE as she wanted to be professional and understand the welfare system. She was also involved in the Salvation Army, Cross Road, and the BEAT (Bridging Education And Training) Programme. She was keen to help and support the children who were under sixteen with a government support program.

At that time, only the church was helping the underage children of the street, so Nora, being a lover of children, wanted the government to set up a support system for those unfortunate children of the street. At the same time, she was interested to set up an Islamic Council of Victoria for the Muslim women in Australia and to set up a prayer room for every university in Melbourne. The Islamic Council of Victoria was set up in 1988. Another subject on her mind was to set up a *halal* food center for Muslims and to introduce the dietary concept of *halal* food to children from young to university level. Nora achieved her aim and her group was called the Muslimah Islamic Group. This group deals with various kinds of Muslim issues, including funeral preparations, which include bathing rituals and burial. The Muslimah Islamic Group also refers to all Muslims, especially the migrants, which include those from Lebanon and its Middle-Eastern neighbors, Somalia and Northern Africa, Malaysia, Afghanistan, and other Muslim minorities living in Australia.

Friendship with the Australian Prime Minister

It was through Nora's position as the vice president of the Muslim Women Council that she met a member of parliament, Mary Gillard, who is a good friend of another MP, Julia Gilliard, who lived at Altona not far from Point

Cook where Nora lives. It was through Julia Gilliard, who later became the prime minister of Australia from 2010 to 2011, that she managed to push through certain difficult issues. Julia had helped her by writing appeal letters personally signed, although the facts on the Muslim issues were compiled by Nora. During Julia's term as the prime minister, three mosques were constructed in Victoria and the Bill of Rights for *halal* food was passed under monitoring by the council. Although an atheist, Julia Gilliard understood the difficulties of the Muslim women residing in Melbourne. And because of her compassion, Nora presented her with an English version of the Koran, which Julia said she would read one day. On the Malaysian prime minister's visit to Melbourne in 2011, Julia hosted a luncheon and invited Nora to attend the lunch in the presence of the wife of the Malaysian prime minister.

Being a community leader exposed her to different religious traditions; for instance, Albanian women after matrimony are tied to the house and not allowed to leave except for visiting her parents and on her own funeral. They are very submissive wives, and if the wives work, the husband is entitled to her money. Once an Albanian woman confided in Nora of her husband's gambling habit that used up all her money. When the husband found out, he threatened to divorce her.

There was also the case of Aiwa, a West African girl who came to Melbourne and spoke only French. Her irresponsible husband, Tahir, left her for seven years as he was living with his business partner. Aiwa approached Nora to get herself a lawyer and get a divorce by Australian law and custody of her nine-month-old child. Nora consulted a sheikh who was a Somali lawyer who was blind and spoke nine languages. Nora later invited him to help with her community work to mainstream Islam to the Australian community.

In the course of her work with the migrant community, she has encountered some light-hearted propositions from a few young men who found her to be nice, bubbly, and accepting. The Egyptian men would tease her about her nice "boobs." One Somali man with eight children once proposed to her in order to start a business by using her position and influence.

The more I spend time with Nora, the more I realize her boundless energy and her compassion for the less fortunate and her endless contribution to society. Through being with her I have met some wonderful children, some of whose parents she knew before they were born. For instance, Maryam, a Thai girl from Afghanistan. Maryam is beautiful, with a petite frame, lovely fair complexion, and beautiful facial bone structure inherited from her Pashtun blood.

She came to Melbourne with her husband, also a Pashtun, and together they worked in Melbourne, making enough to buy a house. They had one son before her husband died of food poisoning. Maryam came under the scrutiny of the Social Security System and Nora opened her house to her. Maryam stayed with the family for a few years. Nora had a girlfriend called Yam, a Singaporean girl who took pity on Maryam and consented for Maryam to be married to her husband, Rashid, who is an Indian by birth but converted to Islam, thereby becoming Indian Muslim. The agreement was that in order not to embarrass Yam and "drop her water face," in the event that Yam and Rashid divorced Maryam would also follow suit; i.e., be divorced from Rashid in order to protect Yam from the embarrassment of being divorced should Maryam remain in the marriage. With this agreement, Maryam left Nora's house and moved in with Yam and Rashid in their house. It worked well in the beginning. Then one day Yam noticed a love bite on Maryam's arm and became jealous of Maryam and had frequent fights with Rashid that later led Rashid to divorce Maryam. They later reconciled to have three beautiful children, Amira, Natasha, and Zahara. Rashid had a heart attack one day and died, leaving Maryam with her four children, who moved in for a few years with Nora until she moved back to her own house, which she bought with her first husband. Nora's daughter Zowie became a foster sister to the three girls while they were growing up and spoiled them with her wages that she earned monthly.

Just a few years ago Nora adopted two Cambodian girls from Malaysia whose parents of Cambodian origin settled in Kuala Lumpur. The mother remarried a Cambodian man who, through an illegal syndicate, sold and sent the two children, Fatimah and Dahlia, and their brother to work on a farm in Melbourne. When they arrived in Melbourne, they were made to stay in a house together with other laborers, some of whom were Indonesian. Fatimah was impregnated by an Indonesian, then one day while traveling on public transport she was arrested for not having her proper documents. She was taken by the police to a social welfare community center, where she and her sister met Nora, who was in charge. Nora agreed to adopt and help Fatimah deliver her daughter, Emily. She was born with an abnormal skull and had to be operated on while she was just a year old. By the grace of Allah, Emily recovered to become a very intelligent and hyper child, and her nonstop chattering amused everyone. Her mother Fatimah managed to get a job at the Sunshine Chicken Factory and took a hospitality course in the evenings. Her sister Dilly met an Australian boy who was a nonbeliever and opposed to the idea of converting to Islam in order to get married to Dilly. But he finally agreed and the pair left to work in Queensland.

Nora's efforts paid off and her selfless devotion to the underprivileged people made her incomparable to many. How many of us would give our time, effort, and means for the sake of making life better for others? One can see the light of happiness shining on her face whenever she spoke of Emily, the granddaughter that she adopted. She was sympathetic to the asylum seekers and wrote letters to authorities in order to ease the way for the hardcore detainees.

In her course of work, Nora has encountered some difficult and amusing situations she had never experienced before, but she was forced to act as a community leader everyone depended on. One such case she related to me was the case of an Indonesian girl who died after an accident in Shepperton. Nora was informed by another Muslim colleague, but she could not go to the emergency room as she was in the middle of a lecture she was conducting. She relied on her friend Ida to do the bathing ritual she herself was obligated to do as a community leader even though she was not a religious teacher. Her friend Ida agreed to do it, but after she plucked some plums from the backyard of her house in Port Melbourne she fell and was hospitalized. Nora managed to get a Muslim volunteer to do the bathing ritual in a truly Islamic way, only to realize later that she had done it on an Australian girl instead of the Indonesian Muslim girl. She only realized the mistake later when the family of the Australian came to claim the body.

When I asked Nora how many children she had fostered, she replied, "Countless." When I asked her again if at all they remember her, she replied not all but her satisfaction was not in receiving but in giving whatever she could to help the less fortunate.

There have also been lots of cases of mental disorder and depression, especially among the Somali women. As in the case of Raziah, who had a nine-month-old baby she could not feed because there was no money. Her husband had many gambling debts and had many people coming to the house asking for money. As a result, they had frequent fights, until one day the neighbors heard a commotion in the house. She had knifed her husband in the face and he fell down in a pool of blood. The neighbors helped to bring him to the Mercy Hospital. He survived the incident but was badly injured. Raziah asked Nora if she could get a divorce from her husband. Her husband demanded that she return the nine camels she was given as a dowry in marriage, which she said she did not receive. Raziah later moved into a neighbor's house but her husband later accused her of sleeping with the neighbor's husband. She was moved to the Refugee Center at Dandenong. Meanwhile, the Somali Community leader insisted that she return to her husband. According to Somali law, a woman, once married, cannot leave her house until she dies and she is confined to the four walls of her house. Nora had to attend with Raziah the kangaroo court, a tribal meeting with the entire Somali community. Eventually, Nora had to appeal to the Australian court to get Raziah a divorce from her husband, which she eventually received.

Nora, having done more than her fair share of charity work, now concentrates on her Migrant Hubs, a café in Werribbee she founded four years ago and where she assembled Malaysian vendors and their specialty food. Jobless migrants are welcome to eat there without any charge because to Nora, "Happiness is a healthy mental attitude, a grateful spirit, a clean and conscious heart full of life and kindness in the ability to love people more than they really deserve." And in Nora's case, "In charity there is no excess but goodness and goodness in nature."

This charismatic wonder woman had chosen life in another country but her own in order to spread her goodwill where she was most needed, unrecognized by her own motherland. However, because of her charitable nature, she is ever willing to be where she is most needed.

Opening of migrant hub

Nora's family

Nora with friends

Nora's adopted children

Chapter 5

THE MISSIONARIES

(a) A Girl From Sulawesi

"A stream always succeeds in forging its own way to the ocean, overcoming all obstacles in its path, with vision and perseverance, so too can we achieve our desired success."

—Anonymous

The island of Sulawesi is one of the islands of Indonesia even though it is situated closer to the Philippines. Its inhabitants are predominantly of Muslim origin. The town of Makassar was once colonized by the Dutch, leaving traces of a mixed generation with fair white complexion and beautiful-looking people of a mixed race. My destination was Surabaya, its sister town of 4,000 people. And when I landed at the Surabaya Airport in 2014, I was impressed by the modernity even though as one passes the road from the airport to the city, one would be able to see traces of the old Surabaya. As the name suggests, Surabaya is the home of peasants and farmers of the 250 million population of its motherland, waiting to be developed alongside its richer capital city of Jakarta. It is an old city showing the old civilization: dilapidated old wooden houses attractively painted in very light sky blue, old women on the street shoeless, and paddy fields in sight. This is the picture of the old Surabaya that I would love to capture, because despite the ruins of the dilapidated buildings and paddy fields and many mosques with colorful domes interspersed in between the villages. It is a picture of charm and naturalness that became the artists' impression and general character of this romantically named city. The roads are wide unlike in Bandung where I boarded my flight, which is a holiday resort with beautiful cool weather unlike anywhere else in Indonesia and a favorite destination of golfers from the mainland and elsewhere. Bandung, in contrast, despite the narrow roads that attract traffic congestion, is a bustling city of many restaurants and shops selling clothing, and is definitely a shopper's paradise. Having passed through the old town of Surabaya, I was surprised to find my hotel to be very luxurious, with a five-star shopping mall next door. "Who on earth can afford to buy these goods?" I said to myself, but not after I saw the new affluent crowd on a Sunday afternoon in the mall. I badly needed a hair wash and was directed to Johnny's, which to my surprise was the second busiest hairdressing salon I have been in years since the one I visited in Beirut many years ago that I rated as the busiest, with one hundred staff attending to clients. I was immediately directed to a chair and served by two young and happy Indonesian guys clowning away in their own language as one massaged my head and the other my feet as a prelude to the hair wash. It was the best hair wash I have had in years because the "Indons" are noted for their good and cheap massage and they would go to all ends in order to please the customer. I couldn't believe my eyes when I saw the bill as it was a pittance of what I would have to pay anywhere else, even in my own country. As I sat for an hour relaxing and enjoying my head and foot massage while being amused by the behavior of my two attendants, I began to notice the young people around me, which interestingly resembled the youth culture of any big city. The only difference is that amidst the poverty of the 250 million population in Indonesia, there is a segment of the old rich and the *nouveau* rich parading their wealth in the most ostentatious manner. One very pretty and young Indonesian girl of very fair Indon-Dutch descent walked in wearing a silk blouse and faded jeans purposely torn at the knee and wearing three beautiful and expensive antique rings on three of her fingers, and taking a photograph of her own face with her latest digital camera as the attendant washed her hair. This is the life that Maryati left behind some twenty years ago in order to embark on her own journey of self-discovery. And in the process, she found a more purposeful life in another country other than her own, where the mindset of the new foreign people she met matched that of her own inquisitive mind.

As I wandered around the breathtaking greenery of the elegant Borobudur Hotel whilst appreciating the beautiful treasures of Indonesia whose heritage this unique country is proud of, I marvelled at my friend's courage and inner strength which led her to her spiritual journey and discovering her true self.

As I sat with Maryati at our favorite café, Brunetti, on the popular Lygon Street while enjoying the freshly made sandwiches and chocolate éclairs, at the same time absorbing the beauty of the decor of the Italian café and the retro design, she reminisced the old bygone days. The Italians have definitely made a statement in Victoria, where they inhabit most of the expensive real estate. If one were to drive along the coastal route from central Melbourne to Mornington Peninsula, one would notice the beautiful coastal villages with large beach houses along the way right up to Sorrento, which is the home of the affluent Italian society. It is a typical Italian village with branded Italian shops and restaurants where one would see Italian women in their silk dresses and high-heeled Italian shoes. It is a totally different scenario from the normal Australian culture, which is sports shirts and jeans and sneakers, adorning the streets of the Australian cities.

Hotel Borobudur & Borobudur temple

As I sat there sipping my favorite café latte with Maryati, I learned about life in this big city, which seemed safe from the outside, which a visitor like me would never know unless he lives in it or has been living in it for many years. Lygon Street is famous for its average Italian restaurants that most Italians love to visit. The buildings, except for this famous Brunetti Café, are old and nondescript, only adorned by its decor, unlike the buildings in Paris or Vienna where one can admire the architecture of its facade. At Brunetti, one can see the higher class of Italians dressed in their locally produced merchandise of silk garments and enjoying an Italian lifestyle. I was informed by Maryati that just a month ago there had been a shooting at Lygon Street, as is prevalent in the streets of Naples in Italy or any other gang-ridden street anywhere else.

As we were chatting, I noticed how attractive Maryati must have been when she was young. Although she still retains her good looks, she is always adorned with a *cador* or headscarf covering her hair. She has a typical Indonesian look, tanned complexion, well-shaped lips that showed beautiful white teeth whenever she spoke, thick eyebrows, and her eyes displayed deep pupils. When she was a young student studying in Russia, she could be mistaken for a Chechen girl from the Muslim state of Russia. Maryati speaks clearly, in a nice, controlled, high-pitched voice, expressing her words clearly in well-spoken English with some Australian slang, like "no worries," typically Aussie. Her cheerful personality and positive nature and willingness to give a hand to others are her best traits, and coupled with her intellectual knowledge, made her a pleasant companion.

Maryati is only forty-three years old and married to Joe, an Australian convert of Irish descent, and together they have five beautiful children, whose names are all from the Holy Quran and have a special meaning. Her eldest child and daughter is called Amatullah Kawther Abdullah, *Amatullah* meaning servant of God the Almighty, and *Kawther* meaning a fountain in paradise. Her second daughter is called Sasibil, meaning a river in paradise. Her third child, a son, is called Abdul Rahim Gibrail, meaning a servant of the Master. *Gibrail* is the name of an angel. Her fourth child and daughter is called Tasnim Amatullah Karim, meaning a flower in paradise. And her fifth child, a daughter, is called Amatullah Raihan Beatrice, meaning a tree in paradise. And Beatrice, incidentally, is the name of Joe's grandmother, who worked in the Catholic Salvation Army. Joe's grandmother used to keep coins in a jar for her youngest grandchild to be born, but sadly she died before Raihan was born. Maryati, a bright girl, graduated from the Monash University and had come to Melbourne some twenty years ago looking for knowledge. Now her life basically revolves around her five children, whom she and Joe brought up in a true Islamic way amid a non-Islamic culture. Her eldest daughter started wearing the *hijab* like her when she was ten years old. Maryati teaches at the Islamic school for children in Werribbee and conducts religious classes at the mosques in the evenings, where she is able to mingle with the Islamic community in Melbourne. Maryati herself is a strict Muslim and on two occasions while I was with her she stopped the car and did her prayer on the side of the road, on a mat that she always carried in the back of her car. Another incident was at a cinema when she excused herself in the middle of the movie to pray at the back of the cinema seats. But there is another side of Maryati, who has adopted Western ways, unavoidable as the other half of her is Australian, being married to Joe and his family, whom she and the children are close to. She calls her mother-in-law Patsy and her father-in-law Ian. Joe's family is quite internationally knit as Joe's brother is married to a girl of Indian origin. According to her, in the beginning there had been a little racial tension within the family, and during Christmas dinner, once a year, Patsy, her mother-in-law, had to segregate the dinners.

Maryati got on well with Joe's family, who loved their grandchildren's visits, giving her time to be with her friends and to have time to herself and Joe. Joe's work takes him long distances for days, and once a week she and Joe would go on a date for a few hours to a nice restaurant without the children. But according to Maryati, they do feel guilty for switching off their telephones for a few hours, even though the children were safe with their grandparents who doted on them. When I asked Maryati how the average Australian reacts to her wearing a *hijab*, she replied it was not a problem in the educated areas where she worked, like in the university, as it is accepted. But she does have problems in the less educated and rough areas of Melbourne, especially after September 11 incident and the Bali bombings. As she was driving her car with her daughter two years ago, both of them wearing *hijabs*, a car drove up to them and stopped right in front of her car, blocking her access. The action was just to threaten her as the car drove away.

Maryati, from her twenties and after meeting Joe, had submitted herself to the Islamic way of life and living in a foreign land where her faith was only accepted by a minority. It is her personal struggle or *jihad*, as she understands it to be, and she has chosen this path without any major struggle. She and her daughters, once they come of age, go around dressed in robes fully covering their figures, oblivious to the stares of others. She and her family adopt the Islamic concept of *halal* and *haram*, but they also enjoy the way of life and culture that a western country offers. She herself is so western in her mannerisms, eating habits, and thinking that without her robe and veil she could be a westerner.

Maryati was born in the island of Sulawesi in Indonesia, being the youngest of three girls and one boy. Her father was a policeman and her mother was a midwife. While her mother was a practicing Muslim, her father was an atheist. Her parents went through an arranged marriage and there was not much love lost between the married couple. According to Maryati, she learned from her mom that her dad was an orphan and was raised by his sister and went through hardships growing up. Maryati did not have a close relationship with her father because of her parents' troubled relationship, and her mom, she later found out, never loved her dad but stayed in the marriage out of pity for him. The closest relationship Maryati had was with her grandparents who lived at Gillingenge, which was a very clean area near the forest. Her grandfather was the chieftain of the village and the right-hand man of the Bugis king *Tau Manurung*, meaning someone who has descended. According to Maryati, her maternal grandfather was a rich man and owned a lot of land, but lost it in the Dutch and Japanese interventions in Indonesia. When she was a child, she used to hear gruesome stories of the villagers who were being tortured by the Japanese, even some who'd had their genitals cut off. The villagers hated the Japanese then for their cruelty. She also heard of the warrior of South Sulawesi, Sultan Hassanuddin, who used to fight barefooted against the Dutch as well as the Japanese, who were considered whites.

Maryati grew up during the turbulent time when Indonesia was going through the transitional period of government from Soekarno to Suharto in 1970. It was a period of hardship for the Indonesian working class financially, leading to disputes between her parents at home. She decided to leave Sulawesi at eighteen years of age. She had always been a bookworm and kept to herself and enjoyed her own company. After high school in Bandung, she managed to get a scholarship to Australia, where she studied at the James Cook University at Townsville in North Queensland. After one year she moved to Monash University to do a course in the foreign affairs department and pursue her ambition to become a diplomat. Being an avid reader, she had always been interested in Russian history and was well read on the works of Agatha Christie and read *Samurai* and *Shogun* before moving on to Tolstoy's *War and Peace*. She then applied to do Soviet studies, which she managed to do, and read the history of Russia during the time of Peter the Great, who wanted to build the whole of Leningrad, now renamed St. Petersburg, in gold, which led to poverty and eventually the Russian Revolution.

Believing in her books as the window to the world, during her first year at the Monash University she applied to do an intensive course in Russian language in Moscow. When she arrived in Moscow, which was during the transitional period from Gorbachev to Yeltsin, it was a far cry from the pretty picture of the Anna Karenina world that she imagined, but more of a situation from *War and Peace*. The situation was bleak, especially in winter, when she noticed the crowd queuing for four hours in a −12-degree temperature for food. She spent two months in the Moscow University dormitory, one of the two tallest buildings in Moscow in 1992. She and the foreign students were at an advantage as they had hard currency, which was in demand, especially in the black market. They managed to exchange their US currency to get food supplies from the students from Chechnya. The Chechens were from the Caucasian Mountains, a Muslim region in Russia. During the transitional period from Communism to capitalism, it was a trying time for the Russians, who had to trade their possessions in order to get hard currency to buy food. One would find many "intellectual beggars" on the streets, university lecturers who had not been paid for months. Fortunately for the foreign students who were on scholarship and in possession of hard currency, they were able to buy goods, such as good books, from the intellectual beggars at a pittance. Maryati and her fellow students from Sudan and North Korea had a good laugh, she said, as where else in the world could they go to have a lavish meal at a five-star hotel except in Russia, where their US dollars were accepted at a fraction of the actual price. Maryati became close to a Russian student who was studying in the institute of technology, and she visited the family often as he was very close to his mother. He was a bright student, his father being a lecturer and his mother a mathematics teacher. He made his own satellite receiver, which inspired Maryati. As she became close to many Russian friends, she was invited to one of the KGB's *dacha*, which was a summer villa usually hidden within the beautiful forests. The KGB at that time was already becoming insignificant because of the rise of capitalism. Despite the difficulties faced in Russia, for Maryati it was a mind-blowing experience being in this part of the world where almost everyone was academically inclined, even the taxi drivers. Maryati had learned Russian and was able to converse in the Russian language. English was the least spoken language there, French and German being more common. She used to go to the markets at the train stations where the lecturers were selling watches, books, etc. The vendors were all educated beggars ready to trade their possessions in exchange for hard currency to buy their basic necessities. One day Maryati met a lecturer with little money at a bus station and he was offering the foreign students his time for tutoring at USD 1 an hour. In the course of her stay, she met many Russian students curious to see the outside world. Once at the market she met a Russian lady who pleaded with her to take her out of Moscow. Maryati remembers the tears in the old lady's eyes when she explained that she could not do so. She had the experience of her life in Russia, a country that fascinated her for many years and which she had the opportunity to visit. Although life was not easy during the Communist era, and the winters severe, it was still an enchanting country with a certain charm that one cannot forget. She left Moscow after finishing her studies there and moved on to Holland, where she pursued a hippy lifestyle and did all the imaginable things in those days that young, free western teenagers did. One day, on a train from Luxemburg to Amsterdam she met a foreign guy who just converted to Islam in Turkey, and they started a conversation where he was telling Maryati all the beautiful things that he learned about Islam. That shook up Maryati, and when she returned to Melbourne to continue her studies at Monash University, the experience continued to haunt her as she was not a practicing Muslim. While at Monash University, she met an Englishman who the Aussies, in those days, referred to as "prisoner of the monarch." Andrew was a widow and an atheist who was studying computer science and later worked in a computer company. Maryati was still questioning religion and was practicing the teachings of Buddha until she met a revert by the name of Aminah Vandraft who made her curious about the religion she was brought up in Sulawesi but never practiced. Aminah was introduced to her by an Afghan friend, Zaharah, who was also searching for Islam, and together they started the Islamic Society at Monash University. They introduced a study circle and together they discussed controversial issues on Islam until they found the answers to their long-held doubts on the "new religion" they adopted. Maryati threw away her hippy lifestyle and learned the *syahadat* and went to the mosque on Jeffcot Street to practice her obligatory prayers and started teaching Muslims at Monash University. Gone were her wild days and her questioning of Buddhism, Hinduism, and Catholicism, to which she almost converted, having gone to church often with her Catholic friends.

While she was teaching at the Islamic school in Melbourne, she shared room at Caulfield with a girl called Aishah who was married to a Moroccan man. Aishah had earlier been married to a non-Muslim man and had four adult children, but she remarried to a Moroccan man and had three more children and she did not want to have more. When Maryati later on went to Egypt to study, Aishah frequently proposed to Maryati to marry her husband, who was in Egypt, and be his second wife as she was fond of Maryati. Aishah was forty years old, and although Aishah's husband was thirty-six years old and good-looking, Maryati was twenty-eight years old and unattached, she did not entertain the offer of matrimony. Although Maryati and Aishah's husband shared the same interests as both were into computers, Maryati did not find it right as the idea was mooted by Aishah and it was not a love relationship. In Egypt she met many friends who were involved in bigamy, such as Salmah, who flew to Egypt to be with her husband-to-be from America in order to be his second wife. Another Australian Caucasian friend of Maryati became the third wife of an Egyptian man.

Maryati became active in the Muslim Association by giving lectures and doing class activities for Muslims at the mosque on Jeffcot Street. Later she went to Jordan to learn Arabic and teach English in Islamic schools. She met many Palestinian activists and joined the International Muslim League to lobby in the United Nations for Muslim women's welfare in third-world countries. She also met many students from South Africa who came to Jordan to study the Arabic language. Maryati went with them to Amman, Jordan, where all Muslim women leaders from European, African, and Arab countries came to discuss topics to be presented to the United Nations' meeting in Beijing. The topics were mainly issues faced by Muslim women in third-world countries. Maryati stayed with some North African students, which later gave her the opportunity to visit Sudan, where she continued her Arabic studies. In Sudan she became the guest of the Vice President's wife, who was part of the United Nations delegation. She found North Sudan to be an interesting place and Khartoum being a Muslim country that adopted *shariah* law. She found the city safe and the people helpful, even offering to take her to places. She found a technical job and enjoyed interacting with the local people, whom she found very different from other nationalities and very generous but laid back. She was also most impressed by the cleanliness of the city.

From Sudan she moved on to Egypt, where she met some students from Singapore and moved in with them. She found work in a paper-manufacturing company and at the same time enrolled herself at the Al Azhar University for Islamic studies and the way of life of Islam. However, being a traditionalist in the Muslim teachings of Islam, she found the Egyptian way of life in those days too modern for her newly acquired way of life; for instance, the lecturers at the university were not properly attired with a *hijab*. It was contrary to what she had learned by the book, and she and another convert friend called Rosy decided to leave after having several arguments with the teachers. She was also unhappy because there was no free mixing of students among the different nationalities, as the Malaysians and Indonesians and Asians were put in one class and segregated from the Westerners, which to her intellectual mind she could not accept. As the problems escalated, she and Rosy decided to leave Egypt, which at that time forbade Muslim brotherhood. *Shariah* law was only applicable when relating to family members. The teachers of the Arabic Institute were not allowed to leave Egypt to attend a conference in America, and there was a big disparity between the salaries given to the third-world graduates like those from Indonesia and the Philippines and India who were paid EGP 1,000 a month compared to foreigners from the United States and Western Europe and Australia who were given passports and paid USD 1,000 a month. Maryati felt that there was a certain amount of racism and favoritism for the Westerners. For instance, a friend of hers who was a Philippine graduate called Dina held a PhD but was earning one-third less than a high school graduate from America.

She found the countryside of Egypt to be beautiful, and she was also intrigued by the *bourgeois* or the conventionally upper middle-class society, who spoke French as their main language and Egyptian second. The Egyptians are generous people but can be chaotic. It was said that if one could drive in Cairo, one could drive anywhere in the world as you would be driving alongside donkey carts. One could hear the Egyptians calling each other "Khumar," meaning *donkey*, out of agitation. Basically, she found out that the Egyptians are generally tough

119

people but not systematic, and they generally have a lackadaisical attitude. The three most common words they would use are *ma'lesh*, meaning *sorry*; *bukra*, meaning *tomorrow*; and inshallah, meaning *God willing*. Most of the Egyptians were Muslims while many still hold on to their Coptic faith. There were Jews and atheists as well. There are still many remaining places of worship like churches and synagogues left behind from the Nasser administration. While based in Cairo for two years, Maryati traveled to Jordan, Syria, and Sudan, doing her research for her Islamic studies. She loved Syria. Although predominantly a Muslim country, she discovered a little town in Syria called Malula where the people spoke the ancient language of the Bible called Aramaic. She found the Syrian people to be peace loving. And as one stepped into the *souks* or markets, one would imagine oneself centuries back in history. She visited the burial ground of Imam Shafie who was one of the four teachers of Islam, and visited the beautiful Sallehuddin Mosque. Syria was born during the Byzantine period, as one could see from the ancient ruins in the countryside, while the cafés on the balconies near the *souk* would remind one of a Parisian street. In Syria she was working mainly with the people from Damascus University. She did the same in Aman in Jordan, working and at the same time traveling and breathing in the beauty of the old ruins and old palaces at Petra and bathing in the Dead Sea from where one could see the forbidden city of Jerusalem. Her friends in Cairo led her to Sudan, which she enjoyed the most, working and studying at the same time. Maryati, being an independent girl and resourceful, plus her determination and confidence, never had any difficulty finding work in order to subsidize herself. She believed that as long as one had faith in one's work for the sake of Allah, things would always turn out right and the path would be smooth. Having finished her studies in Cairo and having had enough of the bustling city, she decided to go to South Africa to continue her Islamic studies. While studying, in order to earn extra money she gave religious classes to young children. In the meantime, she was always in touch with her friends in Melbourne, who at that time were planning to match her with an Australian who had converted to Islam a year previously. One day, someone from the university told her that someone was going to telephone her from Melbourne.

Joe had worked as a chef before his conversion and kept a nice collection of wines and spirits. He threw this away after his conversion, which baffled his mother, who said that he could at least have passed it on to her to be given away as presents. But Joe, being a new convert, believed that if it was not good for him, it could not be good for anyone else. So he and his mother had a little disagreement and he thereby decided to go to South Africa in order to check out the girl he had been in touch with on the telephone, and whose picture he had seen from a mutual friend, Aminah. When he arrived in Durban, Maryati giggled when she saw him in his *tabligh* robe and thick beard as he had been mixing with his *tabligh* friends in Melbourne. It was a mix of Adam Ant and Cat Stevens, and displaying a slacker attitude. Maryati thought, "No way am I going to marry this guy."

After Joe flew to Durban to claim his arranged bride, Maryati did a lot of special prayers and *doa* in order to ask Allah to show her if this was the right man for her. Maryati fell in a deep, peaceful sleep from the excitement and decided to accept Joe's hand in marriage. They were married on the twenty-seventh day of Ramadan, which was a year after Joe had converted to Islam. They moved around Durban and Port Chapston, where they stayed in a room overlooking the beach and they could see whales and dolphins from their bedroom. After touring Johannesburg, which was named the second most dangerous place after Los Angeles and where almost everyone carried a gun for self-protection, they went to Pretoria, a quieter place where Maryati resumed her Islamic studies at the university and Joe helped his friend in a bakery, before they finally headed home to Melbourne. The news of Joe's marriage to Maryati reached their Muslim circle of friends in Victoria where they lived. They met up with old friends Nora and John, also a convert, who had told them that they were also going to arrange the marriage between them, but Nora could not find Maryati's telephone number.

Joe and Maryati's marriage was welcomed by Joe's parents, Bob and Patsy, who were curious to meet their new Monash globetrotting daughter-in-law, although the same reception was not experienced with the whole family circle as there were still traces of racism in Australia after 9/11 in New York and the Bali bombing episodes.

Back home, Joe continued to work as a chef on call where he cooked for various foreign visitors, especially the Middle Eastern visitors, at their residences or hotels, while Maryati pursued her career as a teacher at the Islamic College in Broadmeadows, a county in Victoria. In 2000 the college where she taught was renamed the North Western Islamic College as it was overtaken by the Miligurus or the Islamic Party of Turkey and launched by the then Prime Minister of Turkey. The college housed 80 percent Turks, 15 percent Arabs, and 5 percent Eastern Europeans. Maryati and Joe embarked on their first trip to the Holy Land of Mecca to do their *Haj*. In 2001, their first child Amatullah was born. After their return from *Haj* or the pilgrimage, there was a call for professionals to rebuild Afghanistan after the Cold War, where roads needed to be built and infrastructure improved. Ninety percent of Afghanistan was run by the Taliban while 10 percent was still being supported by the Northern Alliance of America. Joe and Maryati, fresh from their pilgrimage, decided to respond to the call to rebuild

Afghanistan led by an Egyptian professor, Yusof Al Kardavi, who wrote on "*Halal* and *Haram* in Islam," meaning the "dos" and "don'ts" in Islam, together with Professor Jamal Badawi.

In 2000, when Maryati was seven months pregnant with her first child, she had a bad car accident. The car was totally wrecked but she was fine, although she was on crutches for some time and had to wear a brace for her neck. After she delivered her first child, Amatullah, she fell down the stairs, but both she and her daughter were saved. Nevertheless, Joe and Maryati decided to answer the call to rebuild Kabul and left Melbourne with their own savings and their two-month-old baby girl, on a mission to set up a school in Kabul. Because of her earlier fall, she was in constant pain and had to hire a servant to do the daily chores. Afghan maids were cheap and easy to hire. The maid was fifty years old and had survived two wars in Afghanistan. She became Maryati's eye to the new world and it was through her that Maryati learned a lot about Afghanistan and the politics involved.

Afghanistan was a big and beautiful country, full of palaces of the Shah of Afghanistan before the war in the 1970s. The affluent people in Kabul lived in large six-bedroom houses with big swimming pools and huge fortresses and high fences. The women were very modern and fashionable, beautifully adorned and wore stiletto shoes wherever they went, a habit still seen on the Afghan women now. Kabul used to be a city of grandeur as Afghanistan used to be one of the countries on the Silk Route where in the sixties opium trade flourished. It was referred to as the Paris of the subcontinent and goods like gold, silver, crystals, and carpets were traded on the Silk Road. Just ten minutes out of Kabul one would see the cliffs made of granite and marble. It was no wonder that the big sovereign countries wanted to capture a piece of the cake. After America invaded Afghanistan, the big palaces became the Pentagon for the American soldiers' military base. The Afghans only know all foreigners as "Arabs" because of the long association with the *mujahiddin* during the Cold War. During Maryati's stay in Kabul, she did not witness any execution or shooting of women by the Taliban as reported. Maryati's recollection of Afghanistan at that time was that despite the hardship suffered by the local people, the foreigners, including her and Joe, managed a better life as they were able to buy themselves carpets for the house and a refrigerator to store perishables in. There were plenty of restaurants and kebab shops and food was not scarce. The Afghan women wore stiletto heels everywhere, just like in Saudi Arabia, Jordan, and other more affluent cities, and there was a school run by Osama Bin Ladin's wife and daughter.

In 1973, King Zahir Shah, who had ruled Kabul for forty years, was overthrown in a bloodless coup. His cousin Daoud Khan, who was the prime minister, led the coup while the king was getting medical treatment in Italy. Afghanistan was now a republic and Daoud Khan became the president while there were rumors that the Socialists in Kabul helped him take power.

Kabul, the capital, was known to be so beautiful that the Moghul emperor Babul wanted to be buried there. It is surrounded by mountains: the Asmai Mountain, the Ali Abad Mountain, and the Shir Darwaza Mountain. There is a university at the foot of the mountain. One of the wealthiest areas is called the Kocheh-Morgha or Chicken Street, which is a narrow, crowded bazaar within the neighborhood. The women in this part of Kabul were a different breed from the women in the poorer neighborhoods where most of them were fully covered. The women here were called modern Afghan women, married to modern Afghan men who did not mind that their wives walked among strangers with makeup on their faces and no cover on their heads.

The Pashtuns are a race from the northwestern part of Afghanistan, somewhere between Afghanistan and Pakistan where the British never had any control and the people were mainly the supporters of the Taliban. Meanwhile, the Northern Alliance was an Afghan group who supported America and was led by Masood in Kabul. In 1990, the Taliban and the *mujahiddin* were left behind and married the Afghan women. Later in 1990, there was a vacuum of power in Afghanistan and the students in Pakistan decided to form the Taliban while the CIA was still fighting the *mujahiddin*. The Taliban would not allow foreign journalists to come into their country and thereby an American lady journalist by the name of Yvonne Redley was captured and later released on condition that she read the Quran and study Islam. The Taliban only allowed Muslim tourists into Afghanistan back then and Maryati later befriended Yvonne Redley and listened to her stories. Maryati was put to work in a women's school and they met many volunteers from all over the world funded by their own country's organizations. Suddenly with the occurrence of 9/11 and after the bombing of Kabul by the Americans, matters got worse when the Taliban refused to hand over Osama Bin Ladin. Just before the bombing, Joe and Maryati decided to pack their bags and leave Afghanistan because of the sad state of affairs that they could not cope with. The roads needed mending and there was no proper hospital for their daughter, and they were also running out of funds as they were not funded by any organization. To make matters worse, communication was bad and Joe's parents, after not receiving news from Joe and Maryati, decided to contact the Department of Foreign Affairs. So after two years in Kabul, Maryati and Joe decided get help to rebuild the poor infrastructure and improve education through missionaries or volunteers in order to rebuild Afghanistan. Traveling in Afghanistan was tough because of the lack of infrastructure. It took one hour to travel ten kilometers as the car had to cut through granite stones and hard marble. It took Maryati two whole days to reach the northwest of Pakistan in order to leave Afghanistan. There she met many other foreigners like her trying to make an exit. The Taliban government had an embassy in Pakistan that issued Taliban stamps on passports for people leaving the country, thereby making it difficult for foreigners to leave the country. Joe managed to smuggle Maryati and Amatullah out as Afghans, although he was trapped and had no choice but to remain in Pakistan. As Maryati was leaving the border between Afghanistan and Pakistan, she could see the Americans bombing the country and she had to stay in bunkers until it was safe. Once out of Pakistan, she went to Singapore then Malaysia, where she was given refuge by a friend of Nora, her Malaysian friend in Melbourne. Patsy, her mother-in-law, and Joe's brother Ian came to persuade Maryati to return to Melbourne with her daughter Amatullah. Maryati returned to Melbourne to stay with her parents-in-law but lost her memory for a certain time. In the meantime, Joe was trapped in Afghanistan. Maryati did not see Joe for two years, although she had a call from him while she was in Malaysia before coming back to Melbourne. At times Maryati had given up hope and accepted the fact that he could be shot dead, while in other times she was hopeful and wished that "no news is good news." It was a terrible time for Maryati as she heard that the Northern Alliance, who were Afghans who supported the Americans, were known to burn enemies alive, and she was worried for Joe. Maryati continued to write articles about Islam and teaching women about Islam. In Melbourne, the newspaper branded Maryati as a sympathizer of the Islamiyah leader Abu Bakar Bashir. After the Bali bombing, Maryati's house was raided. One day Patsy received a call from someone from BBC informing her that Joe had been taken to Guantanamo Bay from Bagram Prison in Afghanistan. Patsy rang the Department of Foreign Affairs to verify the news and was later told it was not true. Later it was learned that when he was boarding the plane from Karachi to go back to Melbourne he was arrested after the CIA ordered the Pakistani police to arrest him, and he was sent to an underground prison, the whereabouts of which were undisclosed. Joe was arrested at Karachi Airport in January 2003, and returned to Australia five months later. He was alleged to have traveled to Pakistan in March 2001 where he undertook training at Al-Qaeda's Al-Farooq training camp in Afghanistan. He was also alleged to have accepted money, a sum of USD 3,500, and an airline ticket to Australia. Joe had served three months in solitary confinement in Barwon Prison's high-security Acacia unit, in addition to the five months he was held in Pakistan.

Joe's Story

According to Joe, he went to Afghanistan in early 2001 to fight with the Taliban against Northern Alliance forces to end a civil war. Jack said he was disillusioned with the Taliban and was preparing to leave before the September 11 terrorist attacks in the US and the US fired the war on terror. He said he went to Afghanistan a boy and came back to Australia a broken man, and was now trying to put his life back together. He said terrorism was totally against every core value, every bone in his body to ever hurt innocent people. As a Muslim he would be the first to stand and defend this country just as an Australian would. He added that politically and religiously motivated terrorism targeting civilians was a crime. He also reiterated that his only crime and stupidity was to get the Taliban visa, referring to the frequent false document charges after he tried to use a fake Pakistan passport in order to leave the region after the September 11 attacks. After his arrest, he spent five months being eaten by mosquitoes in a tiny Pakistan cell while being beaten by the ISI as the CIA or other US investigators looked on. He claimed to now suffer post-traumatic stress as a result. Joe was convicted in the Supreme Court for receiving funds from the Al-Qaeda terrorism network and for traveling on a falsified passport. He was sentenced to five years in jail with a two-year nonparole period. In an interview with *The Age* before his trial, Joe said he traveled to Afghanistan because he was curious about the possibility of a pure Islamic state. He was quoted to say, "You are not going to understand it, and 95 percent of the Australian population are not going to understand it. I was going to see for myself whether the ideal Islamic state was being created." He was charged with receiving money from Al-Qaeda and providing resources to assist in carrying out terrorist acts overseas and in Australia. He was also charged with the relatively minor offence of possessing a falsified passport. He denied having anything to do with the Al-Qaeda, although he was again quoted as saying, "I had plenty of opportunities, sir, but I won't do it because these people aren't on the tram track that I was on." After the verdict, the QC for Joe, unsuccessfully tried to have him released on bail and Joe served three months in solitary confinement in Barwon Prison's high-security Acacia unit in addition to the five months he was held in Pakistan.

In the meantime, while Joe's trial was going on in Melbourne, the local paper in Makassar where Maryati came from quoted an Australian newspaper saying that she was allegedly linked to Jemaah Islamiyah, an Islamic organization linked to many terror attacks, such as the Bali bombings in 2002 and 2004. By quoting the August 30 edition of *The Australian*, which said that Mr. Thomas' marriage to Maryati was the beginning of his link with Jemaah Islamiyah, a local newspaper in Makassar, her hometown, provided a sensational headline to its readers. Maryati's friends and family were very concerned about the false report with the media coverage, especially as later on the accusation was reported to be a mistake and that the Indonesian Foreign Ministry had clarified that she was clean. But the media had done its damage and her friends questioned the media on the impact of the story and the psychological effect it had on Maryati and her family. Maryati's case is a good example of another aspect of the global war on terror. Heavy security measures often end up labeling innocent people as terrorists.

After Joe's release from prison, Maryati and Joe tried to put the past behind them and concentrate on a new life with the children's interests as priority. With Patsy and Bob and Joe's family's support, Joe was nursed back to normality. In her melodious voice and her accepting manner, combined with her strong faith in Allah's will, she cited a proverb related to the events of her life: "Time is like a river, made up of the events which happen, and its current is strong. No sooner does anything appear then it is swept away, and another comes in the place and will be swept away too," by Marcus Aurelius Antoninus.

Her eldest daughter, Amatullah, is grown up now and in her early teenage years. She helps look after the other four children as a substitute mother. Maryati has taught her children independence from a young age and to learn to take care of themselves. Every summer, Patsy and Bob and Joe's family would go to stay in their caravan for a few months in the fishing village of St. Leonards. There, Amatullah and Salsabil, the two older girls, would excel in their water activities, such as swimming, diving, and water skiing, like most Australian children. They have just registered in the village school during summer where Maryati volunteers for the school. The children are free to cycle a few kilometers on their own to school and be by themselves in the summer chalet whenever Maryati and Joe were away. St. Leonards is a beautiful, serene place with long stretches of beach. As one drives along the main road, one would see very tall trees lining the roadside and beautiful beach houses on one side of the road belonging to the fisherman in the community. The children mix well with the locals and the past incident was put behind as they started life again.

With Maryati, I got to see the interesting parts of Melbourne as a Melbournian, such as the once hippy area of

Fitzroy and the unseemly red light district of St. Kildare Beach, Sydney Road, which is the home of middle-eastern cuisine, once the haunt of the drug king Mokbel, and the huge and expensive houses along Brighton Beach right up to Port Melbourne, where we both would enjoy our favorite cakes at the cafés of Acland Street. Maryati knows every little part of Melbourne as she has been there for more than twenty years and had lived in different areas. She showed me the old cowboy town of Williamstown where Joe grew up in a typically Australian house with an intricately designed exterior typical of Williamstown houses.

As I sat reminiscing on Maryati's eventful and fulfilling life, I could almost hear her melodious voice as if singing to me:

"Swing low sweet chariot
Coming to carry me home
I looked over Jordan and what did I see?
A band of angels coming after me
Coming for to carry me home."

And for Maryati now, Melbourne is where her home is.

Indonesia

Surabaya

Maryati with daughters

St. Leonards, Victoria

Chapter 6

THE MISSIONARIES

(a) Doris The Doer

Doris was born Ooi Kim Hoon. Daughter of Senator of Parliament Dato Ooi Eng Hong was how she liked to be introduced. She was a true Malaysian. Titles and positions play an important role in the social life of the small community of people in Kedah, a state in the north, where she was born. She came from a family of ten siblings, five boys and five girls. Doris was very proud of the state where she was born because this is the state of the icons of Malaysia. The first prime minister, Tengku Abdul Rahman who was a Kedah prince, was born there and was instrumental to the independence of Malaya from being a British colony. Another powerful prime minister, Dr. Mahathir Mohamad, who ruled for twenty-two years and is well known globally, also were from Kedah. The twice-nominated king of Malaysia also came from Kedah, whose relatives Doris was very familiar with as she and the king's sister were good friends from their schooldays. Another good friend of Doris, Cik Kalsum, also married into the Kedah royal family and remain good friends with her till this day whenever she visited her hometown. After school, she became a teacher at the Convent Girls School of Kedah and claimed to have taught an important Royalty, who was among her students, and a Malaysian entrepreneur, Syed Mokhtar, who has made a big name for himself in Malaysia. It is no wonder that Doris is passionate about her royal town where she grew up and mixed freely with royalty. She learned the royal customs well and knew her place in order to fit in with the royal circle. Doris's teenage years were full of fun and laughter, a disposition that she has acquired for herself, and made her popular with her peers. She was a party girl who enjoyed ballroom dancing, although her curfew was at ten at night, imposed by her father, who was her guardian after the early death of her beloved mother. Doris got married to Henri Foo Ah Fong, her childhood sweetheart from school whose sister she befriended. Both Doris and Henri's fathers were both managers and colleagues of the bus company UTC in Kedah, and both Henri and Doris were teachers, teaching in the same school. When they got married, the Kedah newspaper had the headline: "Teacher Marries Teacher.". Henri had earlier gone to Australia to study architecture at the Kingston College in Melbourne. In the middle of his studies, his father could no longer afford to pay his school fees as he was also keeping a mistress, whom he had brought to meet Henri at the airport when Henri arrived from Melbourne. In order to help Henri, Doris got Henri a teaching job in the same school. They were married for nine years, from 1967 to 1976, and had three children: two sons, Nixon and Dixon, and Nellixon, a daughter. They named Nixon after the former American president as he was born on the same day Nixon was made president. The second son, Dixon, because he was born in December and to rhyme with Nixon's name. Her daughter was called Nellixon because she was born in November and also to rhyme with the two brothers' names.

However, their blissful married life came to an end when Henri died of liver malfunction. Doris believed it to be an act of voodoo or witchcraft. With tears in her eyes, she spoke as she recollected the hard life and struggle she went through to bring up her three children after her husband's death. She had to pawn most of her jewelry given by her late husband, and her late mother's gifts of gold. Her "Daddy," as she referred to her father, was the only one who used to give her words of encouragement and love that held her through the difficult period of her life. He told her that she would be blessed by her late husband for a successful life later on with her children. Her husband had requested before he died that their children should be educated overseas. In order to fulfil her husband's wishes, she decided to visit the old landlady of her late husband, Mrs. Shilcock, who lived at Boxhill in Melbourne. It was with the intention of recovering her late husband's belongings and books to donate to the Salvation Army and the library. One day, through the help of her late husband's colleague, she decided to seek a certain Australian Minister Mr Paul Landau in order to ask for help with the migration of her family to Australia. Mr Paul Landau who was holidaying with his family at Bondi Beach in Sydney came to meet Doris and her colleague and promised to help Doris to migrate the following year as Doris did not want to resign her teaching job immediately and upset her children's schooling. Unfortunately, a few months later Doris heard that Mr Paul Landau died suddenly of a heart attack while playing tennis. Doris's hope of migrating to Australia was doomed. Doris continued teaching at two schools and gave private tutoring to support herself and the children. Doris bought a new Honda Cub motorcycle to take her three children to school. The motorcycle, meant to be a two-seater, ended up being a three-seater for Doris and her family, and little Dixon used to say, "Mommy, we have six legs coming out instead of four." She remembered once being chased by a masked man while she was on her motorbike in the area of Tobiak. Once her motorbike broke down, and not wanting to be late for school, she hitched a ride from a truck carrying rubber sheets. Doris also suffered another disappointment when her younger brother, whom she was quite close to and who helped her sell her rubber sheets from a rubber plantation she inherited from her late husband, suddenly fell ill and died. She had earlier introduced her brother to her tenant, a divorcée and they got married, only for Doris to realize that her new sister-in-law bullied her brother. George used to borrow money from Doris for his own pocket money as all his earnings would go to his wife. On his deathbed, he told Doris that he was afraid to go as he was worried that his wife would not look after their children. With all the misfortune happening in her family, her good friend Cik Kalsum one day decided to take her to a medium to seek some advice about her difficult life. The medium told her that her efforts would only be rewarded through her children and that she would have to work hard all her life and be rewarded only in the afterlife. The medium also said that she would go abroad and thereby fulfill her ambition of educating her children overseas. Although the news made her happy, she could not fathom how she could go overseas and support her children. One day, Doris's friend's daughter married an Englishman and invited Doris to meet her new son-in-law and his father Peter. After listening to Doris's story, Peter agreed to become Doris's children's foster parent and sponsor their move to England.

Doris's ambition was fulfilled at last and that began a lifelong relationship between Peter and Doris's family, who regarded Peter as their foster parent. Peter was a divorcée whose wife left him for another man and he had vowed never to remarry. Peter cared for the children just as they cared for him and Doris would invite him along every year whenever she went back to Alor Star to visit her family and friends. The children went to a local school and Doris learned to drive, sending the children to school and working as a cashier at a handy store, Robert Dyas. She became the favorite cashier as she was very efficient and had the gift of gab when handling customers. She learned to adopt the English endearment "my love" for all her customers, which drew them to her, and she was always very helpful.

She was very excited when one day Prince William and Prince Harry walked into her store to buy a few things. Her children had finished their studies and her eldest son Nixon was a manager at Tesco, and her second son Dixon worked there as well. Nixon married a Chinese girl from Malaysia while Dixon married a Caucasian girl from Malta. Her daughter, Nellixon, married a Hong Kong Chinese and set up a Chinese restaurant in Somerset. Doris now has five grandchildren who are very close to her and are captivated by their grandmother's flair for clothes and jewelry. They often reminded her whenever she forgot to wear her jewelry. Being an independent person, Doris lives on her own in London and managed to get a job as a cashier at Tesco through her son Nixon after Peter died. She works very hard to maintain her lifestyle as she loves traveling, eating out, and shopping.

Doris has a big heart. She is a funny lady with unending stories, and most of the time she is very cheerful and obliging, ever ready to help someone in trouble, the qualities that attracted many friends to her. She's made many friends from all over the world, their addresses she keeps in her little black book. She has a photographic memory and remembers telephone numbers off the top of her head. Her mobile phone is constantly ringing with calls from friends from all over the world, and she is never short of friends and godchildren she had adopted inviting her to their homes. Her best trait is keeping in touch with friends as she would send them postcards from wherever she is. Her pleasant demeanor added to her willingness to give of herself make her a nice and interesting companion as she is interested in everything around her with a zest for life. Apart from her interest in visiting foreign places and historical sights, she loves collecting antique pieces and she is also a collector of stamps, old coins, and thimbles. She is the owner of five hundred brooches, varying in value from cheap to expensive. Her little flat in London is filled with a collection of antiquity passed down from friends she has taken care of. Just as she is fond of antiques and jewelry, she also loves big names and royals. She loves to be around important people and be photographed with them and would go to all extent to impress them. Despite her shortcomings, Doris has the kindest heart one can find in a woman. She became acquainted with a mother and daughter from Iran who were evicted from their homeland and came to live in London. Doris cared for the Iranian mother and crippled daughter when they were finding their way around the unfamiliar big city of London. She sympathized with them when their young son was taken to prison in Iran and their properties were confiscated. When she had to leave London to go back to her hometown Kedah on her annual, leave, she felt responsible for them and invited them both to visit Malaysia. She never left their sight and took them to Melbourne when she visited her old friend, her late husband's ex-landlady who was in her nineties. She once met a Spanish guy in London whose wallet was stolen and loaned him some money. He was eternally grateful to her and invited her to visit him in Spain. She cared for another English lady who lived in the posh area of Kensington in London. She looked forward to Doris's visits and hearing her never ending stories of her life. When the lady died, she left Doris some of her antique furniture. Doris was never predicted to get material wealth by the various fortunetellers that she loved to visit whenever she needed consolation. She was told her only key to her fortune would be lottery tickets, which she would obediently buy every week at a meager cost. But she was told that she would have a fulfilling life and travel many places. She has come to terms with herself and knows that happiness does not always come with material wealth, although the latter is always the tool for measuring one's status or success in life. Sadly, not everyone with material possessions in life is happy. Some people could not handle wealth and fame and meet tragic endings. Contentment is the key to happiness and makes the world a better place to live in. That she learned through her many friends who have left her and became a consolation to her. Her asset is her ability to make and keep lifelong friends and keep long-distance friendships alive, as well as her ability to have a happy life loved by family and friends.

Although living abroad, Doris makes yearly trips back home in order to pay respects at her late husband's grave. Just recently, she lost her eldest brother, whom she was close to and who helped her in times of need when she was in Malaysia. She was very affected by his death as he was the eldest in her family, but she was consoled by the fact that she was able to talk to him on the telephone before he drew his last breath. That is the price of her living away from her family. She did go back for his funeral though. Doris now has PR status in the UK and her children are all British citizens. She has managed to accomplish her late husband's wish that her children be educated abroad through the help of Peter. Before he died, Peter wanted to marry Doris, but she refused out of loyalty to her late husband and not wanting to lose the her husband's family name and her Chinese name.

Doris takes life one day at a time and makes the most of it whenever she can. Her son Nixon calls her every day and she is blessed with good children and grandchildren. She travels to many places with family and friends and receives many guests from home, whom she would take to her favorite restaurants. She enjoys life despite the turbulences in her early life, and she enjoys the freedom of living in another country. As much as she loves her country, her home is now England where her children are, and she is content only to celebrate her birthdays every year in Malaysia and bring all her friends there and have a big party. Her motto is: "What is the use of worrying? It never is worthwhile. So pack your belongings in your old kit bag and smile, smile and smile," by anonymous.

This is a story of a remarkable lady, who despite many pitfalls and disappointment in her life, believe in herself. She is not one to take "No" for an answer and all things are possible with Doris. Her positive nature, sheer determination and willingness to work hard coupled with her compassion for other people has paved way for her in achieving her goal. Henri, her late husband would have been very proud of her accomplishment as a single parent.

As a friend remarked, "There is only one Doris."

DORIS WITH FRIEND, GORDON

Doris The Doer

Chapter 6

(b) My Trip to Moscow with Doris and Our Friends from Far Away

"If only we could go back to Moscow, sell the house, finish with our life here and go back to Moscow."

—Anton Chekhov, 1860–1904

My friend Doris had many times invited me to go to St. Petersburg where she had Russian friends, Nikolai and his wife Adele, who lived with Adele's parents in a five-bedroom house in St. Petersburg. Nikolai used to be a part of Yeltsin's entourage before the Putin administration took over. He has now retired early and wrote a beautiful book on life in a Russian countryside, which he published in America. Adele had been a journalist then, and after the turn of tide, the family moved to live in Adele's hometown near Munich in Germany, so I never had the chance to enjoy the hospitality of Adele's home in St. Petersburg where Doris stayed for two weeks with another friend, Irene. They had such a lovely time enjoying Russian hospitality as well as visiting the beautiful museums and the former winter palace of the last tsar of Russia, now called the Hermitage. Doris talked endlessly of her Russian trip, and when we received another invitation from Nikolai to visit Moscow, I could not refuse another opportunity to visit this interesting city that I was so curious about. We were informed by Nikolai that a Muslim friend of his has offered to look after us during our stay, and it made me all the more curious about the Muslim community in this foreign land. So Doris, Zetty, and I packed our bags from London, all excited to see this new city after the capitalist government took over.

I had actually been to Moscow during the Communist regime some twenty years before, in 1984, to visit my sister and brother-in-law who was working in the foreign service department of the Malaysian government. I recall the Communist times then in this "new city." I was on my way to London and decided to stop in Moscow to visit my sister's husband and family who were serving a "hardship" posting after Tokyo. I remember arriving at the Moscow airport on the Russian airline Aeroflot and being received by my brother-in-law in his Russian-made automobile, a Zhiguli. Although it was May, it was blistering cold, and as we drove along I noticed the scenery was white as the roads were paved with snow. I recall going shopping with my sister to the "government shops," where I was able to buy the best bohemian crystal glasses for USD 2 each. Being an avid shopper, I helped myself to the blue and white porcelain bird figurines and samovar designs that cost me next to nothing but became my prized possessions as mementos of Moscow during the Communist times. A familiar figure in the Russian scene is a *babushka*, an old woman wearing a scarf. *Babushkas* hold an important place in a Russian family as they are the spirit of Russia's older generation, and to a certain extent, the whole country. The Russian mascot or souvenir also portrays a *babushka*. We would pack sandwiches and apples before we set out on our shopping excursion as there were no restaurants or cafés that we could go into on our own as we did not speak Russian. We were invited mostly to the houses of the various embassies but never got acquainted with any of their people as the Russians then were very wary of inviting foreigners to their houses. We saw many men and women belonging to the older generation in the parks or on the streets and life seemed hard. It seemed to me that they belonged to the prewar generation and we saw very few of the new generation there. Only once on our shopping spree was I approached by a young girl who wanted to know where I bought my jeans and my high-heeled shoes as we did not see many shops selling high street fashion for the young aside from necessities and souvenirs.

As a result, after visiting the beautiful palaces and the famous Russian circus, I was happy then to leave Moscow for the more welcoming atmosphere of London in 1984. So my curiosity about the "new city" lifestyle and oligarchs that I read about in novels and magazines made me visit Moscow again, this time under a capitalist government. Stories I have heard of modern Russia astound me. There now seems to be a huge gap as the powerful and connected can rake in eye-popping amounts of money and a USD 275,000 bottle of champagne is on the menu at a Moscow hotel just thirty miles away from impoverished villages. The new Russians are obsessed with status and would ask for the most expensive wine, not necessarily the best. I also read about the new amazing Trans-Siberian Express, the Golden Eagle, a luxury liner offering the best caviar and cabins outfitted with flat-screen televisions and heated floors. A one-way ticket from Moscow to the eastern port of Vladivostok costs close to twenty thousand dollars, and there are Russians who can afford that amount of money nowadays. This is a country with some of the wealthiest people in the world, the so-called oligarchs. They are often shrewd and politically connected individuals who scooped up and grabbed ownership of state enterprises when Soviet times ended.

When we arrived at the Domodevo Airport, while Doris and Zetty were frantically looking for someone to help unload their baggage, I went to the glass door to try and identify our hosts who would be greeting us. I saw a group of men and a Russian lady looking at me, trying to identify me as I was trying to identify them. I recognized Nikolai, whom I had met earlier on his visit to Malaysia, and a young, good-looking man in his thirties whom I thought would be the liaison officer as he stood in front of the others. The rest of the group consisted of a plump Russian man who was a professor, a tall young Russian guy in his twenties who turned out to be the interpreter and was called Dominic, and the Russian lady Olga, a common name in Russia for females, and I later found out she was a teacher. They were hired by our host Mr. Islam, who I thought would be the liaison officer, to take care of us while he made his way here from the Muslim state of Chechnya. We were surprised that our host, whom we expected to be an elderly Muslim man, turned out to be a young man who reminded me of an Islamic scholar back home. This was the first time we heard of the Chechen community in Moscow. He appeared to be very serious-looking though he had a boyish look about him, with an air commanding respect from the people around him. He moved with speed, talked little, and appeared rather shy, but he presented an image of a young, successful Russian businessman. He was dressed in designer clothing and was very much the image of the young and affluent generation of today. But as we got to know him, I realized that there is a certain naturalness about him that came from an upbringing in the countryside despite the new wealth surrounding his lifestyle. He was a strict Muslim, observing his prayers five times a day and fasting twice weekly. We were left most of the time with the entourage that he hired to take care of us, but whenever he could tear himself away from his work he would show us around Moscow in the evenings or take us to nice restaurants for lunch and dinner. With him, we saw places that an ordinary tourist would not be able to see or visit. He drove his latest model Mercedes car, easing his way through the traffic congestion of the city notorious for traffic jams, while shoving a few rubles in hands every now and again in order to manoeuvre his way through.

At first, just as we left the stern-looking immigration officers, we were greeted by our Russian friend Nikolai, a tall and bald-headed man with a typical fair Russian look. His physique qualified him to be a bodyguard in this "mafia" guarded city. With him were several other people who were hired by our kind host to accompany us during our entire stay in Moscow. We later found out that our host and his brother-in-law, called Masood, and another friend called Roslan are from the Muslim state of Chechnya in the Caucasus Mountains, which formed part of the Russian Federation like Georgia before it became independent. We later learned of the federal states of Russia and what impressed us was that they seemed to get on with each other despite some cultural differences. After checking in at the Marriot Hotel, we were taken to our host's luxurious apartment in the nice part of the city, near the Moskva River, to meet his wife and family, who prepared us a spread of Russian delicacies, complete with different types of caviar, a famous Russian delicacy. Islam and his family live in Chechnya, which is some twenty hours' drive from Moscow, in the beautiful countryside, though they maintained an apartment in Moscow for their weekly visits. Masood is an educator and works in a school in Chechnya. Throughout our stay, we were taken very good care of by our host and his entourage as we visited the Kremlin, which is the administrative part of Moscow and where the presidents and previous czars resided. There is also an underground vault near the Kremlin museum where the crown jewels are kept, and it was an eye-opener for us to see the treasures of the former Imperial family. We visited many museums and art galleries where we saw so much history and enjoyed seeing the huge collection of lovely paintings on display. We visited the Moscow University, which is a lovely building and the pride of Russians, as well as the underground stations reputed to be the most beautiful in the world and well decorated with *objets d'art*. We were most impressed with the Russian tour guide that we met at the Kremlin museum, a middle-aged lady, well dressed and as nicely made up as most Russian females, who knew her history off the top of her head and rattled on endlessly about the history of the places we visited. Later on when we got into a conversation and asked for her address or a telephone number for correspondence. She suddenly clammed up as though afraid to commit herself. One of the things we enjoyed most was to sit in the park at the famous Red Square, which was painted red in honor of the war heroes who died fighting for the country, and just watching the new generation of well-dressed Russian females in their silk dresses walking in the park in their stiletto heels on a sunny October afternoon. One evening, Nikolai used his past connections and managed to get us last-minute tickets to see the famous Russian ballet *Swan Lake* at the Bolshoi Theatre. Through Nikolai we met a very nice white Russian family who invited us to their lovely home in the scenic woods of Moscow. Our host was a retired high-ranking officer of the government, having served under a few presidents, the last being Putin. He was very proud to show us his collection of guns and armor, including the well-known Russian made Kalashnikov. Doris and I had our first lesson trying the different rifles. Much to our excitement, I managed to hit the target. The visit changed our perception of the Bolsheviks, whom we regarded before as cold and distant people, especially toward foreigners. What I can say of the Russians is that once you get to know them they are the opposite of what their stern exterior shows. They are very accommodating people, both men and women, and curious to learn about the outside world. Our visit to Moscow was one of our most interesting experiences as we were able to see an old, historical city transformed into a super modern city while still retaining its charm and historical past. The mingling of the population from Georgia, Albania, and Chechnya made it interesting to an outsider. With our newly found Russian friends, we rate Moscow as our favorite city—a city bustling with action and yet retaining the romance of the past. We were astounded by the crown jewels tucked away in the vault in the Kremlin, which used to be the palace of the tsars. The big rocks that we saw fed our imagination of the *bourgeois* times during the period of the imperial family, where the ladies were adorned with layers of pearls of different sizes and the greenest emeralds from the mines in Russia. Russia used to be the richest country before the Russian Revolution, enjoying a *bourgeois* society from the period of the Romanovs to Stalin to Yeltsin and the oligarchs of current administration, which can be seen from the exclusive shops of Moscow, which retail fur coats of mink and sable costing hundreds of thousands of dollars.

The trip has changed our perception of the Russians as being unfriendly people after learning that many Russians develop coldness in public merely as a defense mechanism, suppressing thoughts and feelings and not letting their true self escape. The years of hardship under Czarist rule and Communism have taken a toll on Russian folklore, traditions, politics, and family life till this new generation of more open and mostly well-travelled people.

We thanked our Muslim brothers Islam and his family, who were our hosts in Moscow, for taking good care of us, and Nikolai for giving us the experience of a lifetime in this new, bustling city. We left Domodevo Airport with beautiful memories of Moscow and newfound foreign friends we've kept in touch with through the years since our last visit to Moscow in 2000.

The Moskva River

MOSCOW

A Museum in Moscow

The Kremlin

The Red Square

Chapter 7

THE ADVENTURERS

(A) A Girl from Hong Kong

I first met May at a charity concert at my friend's house, and it was the first time I heard her well-trained, powerful voice singing the song "Evita." Coming from her, it seemed like she was singing about herself. Dressed elegantly in a well-tailored gown, hair beautifully coiffured, and wearing an exquisite set of diamond jewelry to match her outfit, she looked as glamorous as she was normally photographed. As she sang, her expert fingers ran over the familiar keys of the piano, she remembered her lyrics well without as much as a glance at her notes, obviously through years of practice. She was in her sixties then but still looked as elegant as she had in her prime years. I was captivated by her easy charm and disposition. I have heard of her name being mentioned in high-society circles as someone who achieved fame and fortune early in life, but what astounded me most was her multiple talents and her knowledge of music as well as world affairs. She was very poised, gracious, and spoke well on many subjects. She was a very interesting person to associate with. When she finished playing the piano, we got acquainted and I realized that besides being a very knowledgeable woman, she was also very "with it" and had a good sense of fun. She enjoyed being with younger people as much as she enjoyed being with people of her own age. It was as if we brought back her younger days, which she missed, as much as we relished her company and sharing her knowledge on music and listening to her life experiences.

The stories she related to us of her youthful days made us gape in awe at the interesting times that she lived through. We rummaged through her stacks of pictures and albums of the lifestyle she led while she was married to the General, and her travels overseas and the important personalities that she met in her travels and at home. As she told us many times over, she was born at the right place and at the right time when things began, and she eventually reached the top in her own right through sheer hard work. She said that events came naturally into her life and she did not ask for things to happen when they did. The men during her time, she said, were truly gentlemen, whether born or bred, and had a lot of respect for women. That was the generation of not so long ago when the days of ballroom dancing, such as the foxtrot, the quickstep, and the tango, filled her younger days. Those were the good old days, she reminisced, although through her own admission she said that life had not always been smooth and easygoing for her. But somehow she managed to sail through and handled situations as best as she could and picked herself up again all by herself, too proud to ask for help from friends or family.

May Lee, born Li Mei In, was born in Hong Kong in 1938 during the Japanese occupation of Hong Kong during the Second World War. Her mother made her learn to play the piano from an American Chinese lady who was stranded in Hong Kong during the war. At her mother's insistence—something she is eternally grateful for till today—she learned to play the piano at four years old, even though she used to dread the lessons and having to do the finger exercises. She remembered her mother paying her piano teacher with a bag of rice after every lesson. Having mastered the piano, it became a part of her that she could not do without, especially during the time just after the war when not much was happening in Hong Kong. Her being able to play the piano well made her a prima donna at an early age. Her feet barely touching the pedal, she played the "Blue Danube" at her kindergarten school concert. At six years old, she was sent to the Mary Knoll Convent in Waterloo Road in Kowloon from 1944 to 1950 for her primary education. She suffered a major setback in her early life when her parents divorced, creating a scandal in Hong Kong as it was one of the first few divorces among the Chinese community. She was then sent to the French convent, the St. Paul's Boarding School, in Causeway Bay, where she mixed with the children of affluent families who migrated from China. She brought her own piano to the convent so that she did not have to share with other children. The convent accommodated her piano in another room where she could practise on her own for the yearly piano competition. She remembered one of her boarding-school friends who always enjoyed listening to her piano practice, a girl called Lydia Dunn. Lydia excelled in her career after graduating college and became one of the first corporate women. She later became the first lady baroness of Hong Kong, honored by Her Majesty, the Queen. They remain good friends till today. Most of the houses in Hong Kong were big bungalows as there were no condominiums then. May remembered a beautiful house that stood out on a cliff overlooking the beautiful Repulse Bay that belonged to her former schoolmate Andy, whose father, Mr. Alvis, was the architect. This was where the film *Love Is a Many Splendored Thing* featuring Jennifer Jones, who acted as Hans Suyin, and the well-known actor William Holden was filmed.

May recalled going there with her school friend to watch the movie being made. When she was eight years old, she learned ballet at the Azalia Reynolds Ballet School, which was one of the two ballet schools in Hong Kong then. May had so much wanted to be a ballerina when she was young but her height of five feet, six inches did not make it possible for her to excel in ballet, though she did perform yearly with other children at the Shangri-La Ball at Peninsula Hotel, which was the only five-star hotel in Hong Kong then. Another student from the same ballet school she remembered was Nancy Kwan, who had become a celebrity after being chosen to act in another famous movie, *The World of Suzie Wong*.

After her parents' divorce, May's mother moved to Singapore, and May, at sixteen, was sent by her father to visit her mother for only five days. What was supposed to be a five-day holiday turned out to be a fifty-year stay in Malaysia. On the boat from Hong Kong to Singapore, she met twenty Malaysian Chinese men who had qualified as doctors and were on their way home to Malaysia to begin their careers. Her lively personality attracted a few doctors and she received a few proposals of marriage from the eligible bachelors, one of whom was later to become a high-ranking officer in the Singapore government. While in Singapore, she frequented the YMCA youth club, where they had regular social gatherings for young men and ladies doing country dancing; with her mother helping her to get nicely tailored dresses in order to attend the dances.

May loved to dance and she attracted the eye of a Chinese doctor ten years her senior who presented her with a doll on her birthday, a toy she never had while growing up in Hong Kong during the Japanese war. She decided to go to Kuala Lumpur to visit the city before accepting his proposal. His father lived in a bungalow that stood on the same land at the Hotel Equatorial at Jalan Perak. It was a big old-fashioned bungalow with many rooms but had only squatting toilets, which she was not used to in Hong Kong. She worked as a kindergarten teacher in a Chinese school called Yu Der, off Imbi Road in Kuala Lumpur, where she enjoyed teaching the children singing and dancing. Her students learned to sing better and faster than the children of the other class.

She then decided to accept the offer of marriage and to settle down in Kuala Lumpur. Meanwhile, her husband had applied for and was accepted as the Colombo Plan medical officer to work in the first tubercholosis hospital, the Lady Templer Hospital run by Australian doctors and nurses, which specialized in curing many patients of the dreaded disease tuberculosis, which was prevalent then. The hospital met with success when it became the first hospital to perform lung surgeries. May also had her first child during this period, and she had a peculiar craving for crabs, which became her main diet that she consumed regularly at the famous Port Klang chinese restaurant. She gave birth to her eldest daughter in 1957, and in 1958 her husband decided to open a private practice in Kuantan. Dato Lim Ah Lek, a well-known personality in Kuala Lumpur and the son of old family friend Mr. Lim Eng, offered to assist her husband in starting the third private clinic in Kuantan, and they moved to their new house at Telok Cempedak in Kuantan. Apart from looking after her newly born daughter, May was kept busy helping her husband to manage the clinic, working as a receptionist, dispenser, and nurse all in one.

She took a keen interest in medicine while helping her husband, a knowledge that proved useful to her later when she decided to venture into her own skincare company many years later. Sadly, fate had it that the clinic was not to be her chosen lifestyle, and they separated and were divorced a few years later, even though she was instrumental in establishing the clinic's business by getting contracts with plantation companies and the Sungei Lembing Tin Mining Company, among others, through her regular socializing at the Kuantan Club. Being outsiders in a small town, when May and her husband first arrived in Kuantan they were often invited to the palace of the Sultan Abu Bakar of Pahang, where May first met the Pahang royal families and got acquainted with them at the Sultan's birthday celebrations and dinner parties. It was here that she met the prince from Negri Sembilan, Tengku Abdullah, who was the president of the MAYC, a Malaysian youth movement. May later worked for him as his secretary in Kuantan during the day and taught English to adults in the evenings before she moved to Kuala Lumpur after her separation. It was her contact with government officials in the early days in Kuantan that helped her in her travel business later on, as the people that she knew and met then had become high-ranking officials holding important positions in the government.

After her marriage broke up, she moved to Kuala Lumpur and stayed at the YWCA ladies club, which provided reasonable accommodation for people from outstation. It was here that she met many Malay ladies who had come from outstation to Kuala Lumpur to look for jobs, and they became her friends. While living in Kuantan, she had socialized with some government officers and expatriates, one of whom was the chief executive officer of British Airways, who recommended May for a job at the travel office of the Eastern Mining Company as the lady in charge was about to leave her job in a hurry to go back to America because of marital problems. When May went for the interview for the job, she was asked if she could type. She replied that she only knew how to use her ten fingers to play the piano well and she suspected that she could apply them to typing in the same way. She was given the job and her office was based at Jalan Pudu in Kuala Lumpur, next to the French Bank, and later moved to the Merlin Hotel, now the Concorde Hotel, at Jalan Sultan Ismail. The Merlin Hotel in the sixties was the most prestigious hotel in town, and in order to attract a good clientele would change the reception facade every six months. It is also the house of many travel agents, such as KLM, British Airways, and Mahmud Ambak Travel Agent, who were all lobbying for customers. The hotel was well visited by many top government officers as it was the only respectable place to be seen in. Singapore President Lee Kuan Yew was always a guest there during parliament sessions when Singapore used to be a part of Malaysia. May used to enjoy having lunches with her friends every week and they would joke about getting married to a man with a car carrying a flag. Two of her friends actually married men with "flagged" cars, and eventually May too, as her second husband was an army general.

While working with Eastern Mining, May was put in charge of the travel office at Merlin Hotel, arranging tickets for the expatriates of the company as well as its subsidiaries. The Eastern Mining Company, besides mining the iron ore in Dungun in Trengganu, also became a shipping agent for the OSK Line, as well as the agent for Swissair, where May was also in charge of the travel arrangements for the expatriates. May also arranged for the shipping of iron ore from Dungun to Port Klang in Selangor. Later on, when the Eastern Mining Company decided to close its operations in Bukit Besi, Dungun, to return to America, May was offered a partnership by the UMBC bank, giving her 1 percent of the 7 percent commission that the ITA made. May used her keen business acumen and her contacts with friends and government officials, those that she had met earlier while in Kuantan and who have risen to high positions in the government. She made monthly sales of MYR 100,000 per month, which was a lot of money in those days. She started to sell airline tickets to the military and police departments of the government, as well as to MARA and University Malaya. The head of the university then was a well-known professor who was reputed to be a very meticulous man, but May was not intimidated by him as she was used to dealing with difficult people. At the same time, she used to visit the different faculties of University Malaya just to increase her knowledge and to feed her inquisitive mind. She also used to visit the parliament house canteen during the "tea break" in order to deliver tickets personally and to meet her clients. She would enjoy listening to the jokes of the MPs during the break until the sound of bell calling for the MPs to return to their sit-in sessions. One of the MPs she came in regular contact with was her previous boss, the Negeri prince she worked for in Kuantan, and his friend, a young budding politician who was quietly ambitious and soft spoken. She knew in her heart after studying this simple gentleman that he would be a somebody in the future because of his unassuming nature. He would sit in one corner of a room and quietly monitor the situation and use his mind while playing with his Polaroid camera. She felt proud now that the people she knew before and had been her friends on the same level have risen to become people of high calibre and high standing in society. But it was not all work with May, because being a person of many hobbies and interests she would frequent the Selangor Club in order to meet her prospective clients and indulge in her favorite past time, ballroom dancing.

In the course of her work with the Malay State Shipping, the travel agent branch of Eastern Mining in Dungun, Trengganu, she had to arrange chartered flights from Kuala Lumpur to Sungei Besi or back to Kuala Lumpur from overseas. With this experience, she was the first to be contacted by the Brunei Government to arrange a chartered flight from Brunei direct to Jeddah for the pilgrimage. As serious as she was about her business, she loved every minute of it, giving her utmost attention to minor details, which made her popular with her clients. She would drive her clients to the airport if necessary, checked them in, as well as chose good seats for them, and sometimes, she would even ask for their doctor's telephone number in case their children fell sick while they were away. Her nickname "Aunty May" was quite familiar among the children of her clients. Using her contacts in government departments, she managed to secure a contract for senior government officers who were given a free trip around the world with their spouses. In order to entice them, she would offer overnight stays and free hotels while looking after their families in their absence, which they could not refuse.

Sometimes she would come into contact with clients who preferred to fly by jet in order to expedite their travel instead of going by Swissair, which had the reputation for being the slowest and safest. Her company was their agent. She would have to cajole clients by saying that since they spent their whole life waiting for this opportunity to travel, why not go "slow and steady" rather than in a hurry? She would use all her power of persuasion and gimmicks to make her clients happy in order to retain them. With her contacts with the manufacturers in Hong Kong, she introduced the system of giving promotional gifts in order to enhance sales for companies like Lever Brothers and Johnson & Johnson. The promotional items made her earn her first million in Hong Kong in 1960, which she made with her own sweat and hard work, contrary to negative remarks about her by some. She was the first person to start a department store when she went into partnership with a banker on the same premises as the store. Unfortunately, Kuala Lumpur society at that time was a little too premature for such an upmarket retail outlet on the same level as Lane Crawford in Hong Kong, and the business venture did not take off. Her motto in business was that as long as one was hardworking and honest and gave one's best, the rest would speak for itself.

One of the incidents she recalled of her heydays as a travel agent was when she was invited on an inaugural flight to Brisbane. She was invited by the Mayor to promote the Gold Coast, reputed to be a sunshine city. However, the week before she arrived, Brisbane suffered severe flooding and bad weather, with heavy rains and storms. When May arrived at the Brisbane Airport in the heavy storm, she mistakenly went to the departure hall instead of the arrival hall in order to avoid the rain. The mayor had to ask for her name to be called on the loudspeaker before they finally met and she was presented with a tin of sunshine nicely wrapped as a humorous gesture from the Australians.

May enjoyed her work, and with her keen business acumen her earnings multiplied. She invested in her first house built by Selangor Properties. It had a wooden fence, which in those days cost MYR 30,000 per 6,000 square feet of land. With her exceptional sense of decoration, she turned the three-bedroom house into a huge one-bedroom and painted it white. She was living like a prima donna and mixing with the affluent society of Kuala Lumpur. Being very forward and liberated for a new and conservative country like Malaysia, she was sometimes dubbed negatively by the women of Kuala Lumpur society, except for her friends who knew her well. Although she felt that she was being misunderstood, she was a woman who knew her strength and limitations, and she did not let it bother her or pin her down. She was a foreigner living in a new, inhibited society unlike Hong Kong's. Despite this, she made many lifelong friendships among the same group of people who knew her well and admired her for her talent and business ability, being completely independent and a hard worker. The only high-profile part of her life was when she performed for charity events, and through those various charitable organizations that she performed for she became well recognized.

May loved the good things in life she'd been accustomed to seeing in Hong Kong and apart from working, she indulged in her favorite pastimes. Since young she had always wanted to ride horses but was not given a chance as her free time was spent on ballet and music. So after work, she decided to enroll herself at the polo club in Kuala Lumpur to take up horse riding, as it would improve her posture. But after a few falls from the horse, she decided to give up riding totally and go horse racing instead, which was a very popular and upmarket sport in Hong Kong among the affluent society. In those days in Kuala Lumpur, horse racing was a very prestigious event often attended by the dignitaries, such as the Sultan and the Prime Minister. Once a year the club would organize the Sultan's Cup Day, and May used to go with her male colleagues to bet on the horses as she learned to calculate the lucky numbers. One day, she was asked by a certain gentleman how she managed to win even when betting on a three-legged horse. She replied it was not the horse that she betted on but the number and it happened to be her lucky number. She learned that certain numbers were lucky on certain days and she never bet on the condition of the horse as all professionals did. That was how she met her second husband, the Major General. When she was asked what were the qualities that she looked for in a man, she replied, "A gentleman and someone with intellectual capacity, not wealth." She found that in her second husband, and together they shared similar hobbies.

After they got married, they first lived in the Ampang area, a nice residential suburb of Kuala Lumpur, in a beautiful bungalow house on one acre of land leased to her for ten years. The house belonged to the owner of the Cathay Film Organization. There were six houses on the same land with one title and could not be sold to others except the tenants because it was rent controlled. After the May 13 episode, all houses in Ampang went down in value. May decided to buy the house and paid only an MYR 16,000 deposit, which was 10 percent of the total value, and took a loan for the balance. After ten years, she sold the house and bought a piece of land to build her own house on. Because it was an abandoned property, it was shaped like a box. May designed the place to look like a matchbox when completed and named it Camelot. Being very fond of musicals, May went to see the play *Camelot* in London. In the play, Camelot was a place where the winter was never too cold and the summer never too hot, and there was no sadness, only happiness. Being happily married and romantically inclined, May wished for all those good things for her new house. They had frequent parties at Camelot, for which May would go out of her way to make them interesting and fun and with a different ambience. Once, she and the General hosted a King Arthur's Night and she got all the costumes ready for her guests to change into for their respective roles. She got a sword ready for King Arthur to wear along with a bejeweled crown, and the ladies were given flowers to wear in their hair. The King Arthur's Night was held for three consecutive nights, with a different dignitary on each night, the final night featuring the General himself as King Arthur. Every guest was asked to extract the sword from its place and whoever managed to extract it from its position would be King Arthur for the night. In the meantime, the General had a special lever he would push up for whoever he chose to be King Arthur, usually a special dignitary, and he would be the only one able to extract the sword from its position. The room was decorated with wooden tables and benches to set an outdoorsy ambience. There were no formalities between the dignitaries and her other guests. Both the General and May enjoyed giving parties a little extra thought, and every party organized was different. May saw to it that no photographs of the parties would come out to the public in order to protect the important guests, and only those who were invited knew what the theme was or what the party was all about. Although there have been contradictory remarks about the grandeur of her parties, May explained that good parties could be done at little expense with careful planning and getting things cheap. It was, she said, a matter of setting the atmosphere right in the beginning and working hard at it. May took pride in her parties, as she did in whatever she set her mind to do.

Throughout the years May never neglected her music, taking lessons with Gus Styn, a Dutch musical director of Radio Malaysia. Later on, whenever she travelled to London she would take music lessons from Ian Adam, who worked with Andrew Lloyd Webber and coached Sara Brightman to become the star of the musicals *Phantom of the Opera* and *Cats*. He also taught Teresa Tang, the former Tang Lay Kuen, a famous Hong Kong singer, a year before she died. May attended the opening night of the *Phantom of the Opera*, and during the opening scene the chandelier dropped just missing her head before the organizers decided to pull back the chandelier to a safer position. She used to fly in and out of London, attending concerts and musicals, and loved shopping for priceless antiques and chandeliers, which remained her treasured collection. Among one of her most treasured items in her collection is an authentic three-piece silver dish that was a dining table centerpiece, one of only two made, its twin owned by the Johore royal family.

It was also while she was in London that she managed to carry on with her harp lessons begun in the United States with her second teacher, Jeanette Codery, from the well-known Codery family of England. In 1980, the general was invited by the US Army War College to go to Carlisle in Pennsylvania in the United States for a one-year course. Generals from thirteen selected countries were invited to participate, after which the selected officers were destined to move up the ladder in their own country. It was the American way of introducing their country and how their army operated and learn from the participating countries as well. Pennsylvania was the most cultured state in the United States, home to many great musicians. It was here that May first learned to play the harp from a lady of eighty years old and who was the wife of the Philadelphia Symphony Orchestra conductor. According to May, the harp was the most difficult instrument to learn to play and a gold harp could easily cost from half a million to a million dollars, and had to be directly ordered from the manufacturer a year in advance. One plays the harp using only four fingers of both hands, and with the feet moving at the same time in order to change key, unlike when playing the piano.

May also learned tap dancing as she had always been a keen dancer. The first cultural shock she received while new in Pennsylvania was when she and the general received an invitation to a party, which had BYOB instead of an RSVP. She had no idea what BYOB was and she thought at first it was the American way to RSVP. Then she found out it meant Bring Your Own Beer, to which she replied she drank only freshly squeezed orange juice. May never drank beer all her life. She only drank water or orange juice, freshly squeezed and strained until it became as clear as water. So when May gave her reciprocal parties, there was no BYOB written on the invitation. She and the general entertained them with the help of a housekeeper cum cook they brought with them from Malaysia. May participated in all their activities, and before they left to go back to Malaysia the women gave her a farewell dinner without asking BYOB and served her freshly squeezed orange juice.

She related an unusual incident that happened while she was living in Pennsylvania. The telephone number of the house where she and the general lived was only one digit different from the telephone number of the High Court. As May was still running her consultancy business and supplying promotional gifts to companies, she needed to talk to her secretary in Malaysia every morning when it was nighttime in Pennsylvania. The CIA became suspicious of her calls to Malaysia, mistakenly thinking that it was an intruder using the telephone of the High Court office in the late evenings. The CIA were alerted and called the Bukit Aman Police Headquarters in Malaysia to check on May's office number in Kuala Lumpur and its connection with the Pennsylvania High Court. The mystery was only solved when they found out that it was the Malaysian Army General's house number in Pennsylvania and not the High Court's number, and it was actually the General's wife, who was a businesswoman, calling her own office in Malaysia and not a spy as they initially thought.

During the course of her travels, she met important figures like Brian Bryce, who was the president of the Hyatt Hotel chain who, together with Adrian Zecha, who was a friend of May, built the first Hyatt Hotel in Thailand. It was a beautiful resort set up in Phuket Island, but it was built a little too early before Phuket became a "boom" town and resort with many tourists. It was through the Hyatt connection that she met President and Mrs. Marcos of the Philippines and May was invited to attend Mrs. Marcos's birthday concert. Through May's social contacts, she also met the billionaire Adnan Khashoggi, and May invited him to Kuala Lumpur and Sabah, after which he donated a mosque to be built in Labuan. She was invited on his private jet called AK1 to Cannes in France, where he celebrated his birthday on his beautiful yacht. May had a taste of living the life of the rich and famous of the world in her prime. Looking back on her early years, she always had the opportunity to meet people who in later years made it in life. She recalled knowing a certain gentleman from humble beginnings who was struggling with his business selling costume jewelry while she herself was a secretary working in the Eastern Mining office. Today, the struggling businessman is a self-made billionaire because of his hard work and contacts during his early days. It just proves that persistence and diligence come a long way.

May's husband was the Brigadier General in charge of signals for the army, navy, and air force, and colonel in Chief of Signals under the ruler of Negeri Sembilan State, with whom he became good friends in the 1970s and who conferred him the title of *dato* for his services to the country. Although there had been talk among the small society of Kuala Lumpur in the 1970s of the General and May's extravagant lifestyle, May cast those comments aside as she explained that good parties could be given without breaking one's arm and leg. She explained that she came from the affluent society in Hong Kong and wanted to introduce the same affluent lifestyle to others wherever she lived. She was lucky that she found a soul mate in her second husband, the General, and together they shared similar interests for entertaining. They had sixteen years of blissful marriage together, living at their house in Ampang for ten years and later at their own "castle" for another six years. The General's name would always come out in her conversation with others, displaying sadness at his early demise. She said that she had always been afraid that when too much good things were given to her, she knew there would always be repercussion and something else would be taken away from her. She had her own theory that after every sixteen years something would happen to change her life. Looking back on her life, at sixteen years old she embarked on a journey to Singapore, never to return to Hong Kong except on short visits. Sixteen years later she married her second husband, the general. Sixteen years later, he left her to continue her life on her own.

As I sat with May over tea at her house on an impromptu visit, she related to me some stories of her life and entertained me on the piano by playing my favorite song, "Memories" from the musical *Cats*. I wish that I had met this gutsy lady in her younger days when I could have gained some knowledge through her business experiences. To quote her, "You can still make money indirectly by renting a house that you don't own legally, but by renting it on a long lease and doing it up beautifully in order to rent it out at your price." May always had the penchant for decorating and doing up houses beautifully, just as she had the penchant for throwing lovely dinner parties. Knowing May, she could always accomplish whatever she set her mind to do, as she believed that honest work would reap future rewards, and that one should not waste life away but make life richer for oneself by living life to the fullest. Since her husband's demise, she retired from the social life she was used to except to perform for charity events and entertain some close friends who have been with her over the years.

However, her mind is still busy working, and in her seventies she is now building another house for her retreat, for her to use as a concert hall for charitable events and to entertain some close friends. She found a purpose in her late life by giving back the generosity she had been blessed with during her life. She said building the house kept her going as she designed it herself according to her own requirements, as she said who would know your preferences better than yourself. Not even the architect or the builder knows, so only engage them for advice or a second opinion. She kept herself busy by buying the raw materials herself in order to cut cost, thereby learning the tricks of the trade and cutting costs on her house. As much as she is thrifty for herself, she is magnanimous when it comes to doing charity work, and kept on performing for concerts to raise money for different funds. Till 2012, she had been traveling to perform many times in China and Moscow for the United Nations Children's Day. She was invited by her friend the Malaysian ambassador once to perform on Malaysia's National Day in Paris at the Concorde Hotel on the Champs-Élysée.

Once her sanctuary is ready, she has already made plans to organize charity events in her new home for the elderly and handicapped people in order to give them a new hope in life. She realizes the realities of growing old on her own even though she is not without family connections. Her daughter Joanne and her grandchildren are nearby and she sees them regularly. She also still keeps in touch with her siblings in Singapore. But being who she is, she had always been independent from an early age and takes pleasure in living her own life. When asked why she never remarried after her husband's demise, she said coyly that it was not because she did not receive proposals but she did not want her children to grow up with a stepfather and ruin her husband's image. Although modern in many ways, she also had a strict sense of ethics and principles.

Once in a while she would reflect on her young life and the people she used to move around with and now stayed away from by her own choice. With her sharp mind still working, she has some questions to be answered, as once in a while when she moves around with friends she remains in touch with and hears negative remarks about certain people she knew in her past. Being on the outside now, she wonders if people can really change so much with time and circumstances, that the simple people she used to know are not as simple as they were years ago. With this new perspective on her dear old friends, she feels sad for the people she cared about. Maybe she will get the answer to her questions one day, but for now she is busy planning her new house and is still trying to do one or two business deals.

"Life, we've been long together
Through pleasant and cloudy weather
'Tis hard to part when friends are dear
Perhaps it will cost a sigh, a tear
Then steal away, give little warning. Choose thine own time
Say not 'Goodnight' but in some brighter clime
Bid me 'Good Morning.'"
—Anna Letitia Barbauld, 1743–1825

After the concert

Camelot II

May Lee   With her best friend – her piano

To know May Lee is to learn about life in high places and to be able to handle life's challenges and to grow old gracefully. This multitalented lady has left her signature in a country she adopted as her own motherland.

Chapter 8

THE ADVENTURERS

(A) Life Is A Cabaret

"Is it so small a thing, to have enjoyed the sun,
to have lived light in the spring, to have loved, to
have thought and to have done?"

—Anonymous

The streets of Calahonda were hilly and all buildings painted white while the skies were blue, without any trace of clouds all the way from Malaga to Marbella. It is indeed a pretty picture for an artist to paint. Along the promenade of Marbella, one could see the sun seekers and beautiful people walking along in their favorite outfits while waiting to have dinner at the many restaurants along the coast, many of which serve the traditional Spanish dishes of *tapas* and *paella*. *Tapas* is the equivalent of the Chinese *dim sum*, served in small dishes, from different kinds of salads to homemade pasties of calamari and beef dumpling. Paella is the equivalent of Malaysian fried rice, although it is more moist and cooked with seafood. The beauty of the villas and the beautiful weather influence the people, and the lifestyle attracts a lot of foreigners into buying houses as their holiday homes. The whitewashed village of Sitio De Calahonda is situated on a slope and looks very attractive, with beautifully designed little villas, each with its own characteristics. The village is inhabited by visitors who dwell on the Mediterranean climate, enjoying the sunshine and sea breeze while bathing in the blue Mediterranean water. The beaches at Calahonda are not as crowded as that of Marbella, and one is able to enjoy one's privacy for some distance. We walked along the sandy beaches while observing the different nationalities and the young in their pretty clothes on their delicate figures, now a shadow of our past.

Forty minutes away, in the neighborhood of Malaga, is the Costa Del Sol, which has always been a famous and luxurious resort in Spain for the rich and wealthy. Its rival is the Cote D'Azur in the south of France, where rich celebrities gather in the summer for the Cannes Film Festival. In the dock of the famous Puerto Bonus, one could see the luxurious yachts anchored there that belong to the rich and famous, while flashy automobiles in the latest models of Rolls Royce, Bentley, Jaguar, Aston Martin, Porsche, and the like are assembled alongside yachts carrying names like *Lady Gaga*, *The Other Woman*, *Princess*, and many others of the owner's imagination. The beautifully decorated interiors of the various restaurants look very inviting to the passersby, who are always attired in the latest designer fashion, be it men or women, while many yachting agents could be seen entertaining or clinching deals with their prospective clients. It is indeed a world of the rich and famous only known to the privileged few.

Raihana began to reminisce how life has passed her so quickly while the adventures of her youth still remain vivid in her memory. Born from an affluent but conservative background, she had defied her family and peers by choosing to leave the traditional Asian way of life and live a life of her dream. She had always dreamed of being in faraway places and craved her independence and to live life to the fullest. She was able to realize her ambition only after both her parents passed away, and that gave her the ticket to freedom. She left her homeland by ship to embark on the journey that was to shape her future, never to return to her homeland and family. Once in London, she managed to get a job at the Malaysian Embassy as a stepping stone before she joined BBC London. Her beautiful face, well-defined eyebrow, dark eyes with shining pupils showing excitement, and well-shaped lips, as well as her tiny petite frame, were chosen to pose for the BBC calendar wearing a traditional *kebaya*. It became a sensation to her peers in her country. Being a lively personality, she was never short of admirers back home as well as in this foreign land, where in those days Asian girls were a rarity. She was never short of dates, and life indeed was a merry-go-round until she settled down to marry a German man, a decision she made in one of her impulsive moods.

Ana grew up in a little town called KK. Ten years before she was born, her mother gave birth to a son and her father was sent to another town, KT, to work. Her mother, being an outsider in a different state, did not like living in this new town and left to go back to live in her hometown. During this period, her father remarried and Ana only saw her father three times during his visits to see her mother in KK. Ana's mother could not adapt to the situation of sharing her husband, and because of the long separation, she decided to seek a divorce. Ana's mother remarried twice after her marriage to Ana's father, but she never lived in the family house with her new husbands. Ana grew up in her hometown and enjoyed her young life with her relatives from her mother's side. She grew up with her cousins and went cycling everywhere together in their little town. They were called the Three Musketeers by the boys of her hometown. At fourteen years of age, this tiny and lively girl had many admirers, one of whom was later to become a well-known banker, who used to give her free tutoring lessons before he left to pursue his studies in the UK. He wrote to her when he arrived in the UK and asked her to join him, but there was no way she could as she was still studying and her strict father would never send her away on her own. Her banker friend later married an English girl, and that was the end of their relationship. But in Ana's own words, "I would have become a young widow if I had married him as he later died in a car crash back in his homeland." While she was living her teenage life in KK, she used to receive letters from her half-sister from her father's second wife, saying she wanted to meet her. She finally went to Kuala Lipis to visit her father's new family and later on stayed with them from time to time, getting to know her other half-sisters and brother. One day, while on a visit to her father's house, her father told her that her mother was sick from food poisoning even though they suspected it to be an act of witchcraft. She went home to her empty house, only to be told that her mother was in the hospital. Three days later, her mother died. Poor Ana was very heartbroken and mourned the death of her beloved mother, whose company she had enjoyed for the last fifteen years of her life. She then went to join her new family in Kuantan, where her father was serving as the chief minister. She grew up with her half-sisters under the strict control of her father. Because of her father's position, she and her sisters were allowed to join the dancing parties at their house hosted by her father for the British officials. She was intrigued by the life of the Westerners and what she learned of England from them, and yearned to go there and to experience a new life and meet new people.

Ana recalled her relationship with her father to be very formal and strict. And because of his absence early in her life, it was not a close father-daughter relationship. Neither was she close to her own brother, who was ten years her senior. Not long after, her father died of a heart attack while in office, and she mourned the loss of her newfound father who had given her protection and a home after her mother's death. She read the Quran and visited his graveyard often as a dutiful daughter would. One incident she remembered of her father was when a former butler who after years of internalized anger toward her father, who was his master, one day decided to shoot him. At her mother's house, an uncle was visiting her mother and unknowingly sat on her father's usual chair, his face buried in the newspaper while waiting for her father to come down for breakfast. The former butler, thinking that it was Ana's father sitting in his usual place at the table, shot at his target, only to realize that he shot the wrong person. The bizarre incident made headlines in her little town.

After the death of her father, Ana went to live in Kuala Lumpur and worked at the Women's Institute. She befriended an English doctor, who upon hearing of her wish to go to the

UK, told her that he knew someone who was in charge of the Malaysia House in London and might be in a position to help her. As fate would have it, he told Ana to leave in two weeks as another Malaysian Indian girl was also leaving for the UK on the same ship. Fortunately for Ana, she had some money from the sale of land left to her by her grandmother (her father's mother). Her elder brother had suggested that they sell the land in order to get money. Her fare to London cost her over a thousand ringgit then. Always an impulsive person, she packed her bags, told her relatives, and left to seek her new future with excitement in London, a glamorous city she had formed a picture of in her mind..

Her sisters and relatives were spellbound by her sudden decision, but as they knew, Ana was very independent and knew her own mind. Besides, both her parents were dead and her next of kin was her brother, who had his own family, and Ana had always lived on her own in Kuala Lumpur as a working girl. There were many attempts by her mother's relatives to marry her off to suitable men of important families, but none of the schemes worked out. Among her ten half siblings, the one who sought her out then and was closest to her later was to be married to a prince, while the other sisters all led traditional lives, which was not her choice and neither was she very close to them. The boat journey she thought would be adventurous and where she would be able to meet nice and eligible young men as she had seen in films of romantic cruises, turned out to be a nightmare, and she was overcome by seasickness. Her cruise mate though, a beautiful Indian girl who was traveling with her on recommendation by one of the doctors from Mcpherson Catterall and Partners, a famous clinic in Kuala Lumpur run by expatriates, was having a ball of a time and enjoying all the events organized on the cruise. A grand ball for the captain's dinner was organized as they were approaching the Bay of Biscay to give those onboard a good time and to forget their rollercoaster journey. Only eight couples turned up, the men clad in their dinner suits and the women in evening dresses to meet the captain, while the rest of the passengers were tucked in their rooms in their nightclothes, ready for an early night after the rough journey.

Once in London, Ana adjusted well to her new life and stayed at the bed and breakfast youth hostel at Holland Park, a lovely, leafy part of the city. Here she met many foreigners from abroad with her roommate, who was the swinging and beautiful Indian girl who managed to get a job at the Women's Institute office. Together they explored the London nightlife. At that time, young Asian girls were much sought after. Her friend eventually settled down with a nice Englishman and moved to a beautiful house in the countryside, but they kept in touch constantly. Ana always had a penchant for faraway places, especially beach resorts. One day she planned to go with a friend who worked as a dancer to the famous Cote D'Azur, which is the much talked about sea coast of France, a magnet for the rich and famous and celebrities she so often read about in the magazines and novels. In those days, young people would travel extensively, especially from England to Europe and vice versa. All of her pocket money from her work would be spent on holidays as Ana had always been self-sufficient and self-supporting since young. At the last minute, her dancer friend could not take time off from work and Ana had to go alone. She managed to hitch a ride from some guys who were traveling the same way and they dropped her at a nearby port as they were continuing in a different direction. Fear overcame her for once, being in an unfamiliar place, but not for long as she approached an American couple with their child and asked where she could spend the night. They were very kind and helpful, seeing a lost teenage girl on her own, and brought her to a little family-run hotel in a small village near Juan Le Pins, which is a vibrant holiday resort, a favorite haunt of tourists. She shared a room with an American girl who spoke very good French and together they toured Juan Le Pins while visiting nice spots where the young people went. One night, they sat at a nice restaurant while listening to the music of the band playing and noticed a red sports car pass by. The driver was a nice blond, good-looking boy with a poodle as his companion. Minutes later, Ana felt a sensation on her left foot as though someone was licking her ankle, and when she looked down, she saw the same poodle. His master had sent him to make the first introduction. The young man came over and introduced himself and began chatting away in French with the American girl. Not able to join the conversation as Ana did not speak French, she was quite happy to be the third person while the two were having a conversation. To her surprise later, the French guy got up and asked Ana to dance with him and not her friend. When Ana asked him why he asked her to dance with him first instead of her friend, he replied that he preferred her to the American girl. He offered to drive them to Nice where his family had a little apartment and where his brother happened to be staying at that time and the reason why he had to stay in a hotel. He found them a little hotel to stay in Nice, but the next day her American friend had to leave to go back to America. As she was left on her own, the next day she took a walk on the beach and was approached by two well-dressed men who offered to show this lonely young girl the sights of Nice. They brought her to a nice five-star hotel, and who might you guess was there? It was Ana's friend Jacques, who disapprovingly told her that the two men were pimps looking for girls on their own. He told Ana to disassociate herself from them, which she immediately did.

Jacques took her around Nice for the rest of her stay, and it was one of her most memorable holidays in her youth whenever she recalled her young days. Back in London, life was full of parties and Ana was known to only date foreign boys as she did not want her name to be circulated among her own people. She went on another holiday with a French girl to Spain, to Costa Bravo, by train from London. They stopped in Paris to meet her friend's German boyfriend, who worked at an art gallery. They stayed at an apartment for three people for two nights. They were invited to a party of another German guy called Christian who lived in Montmartre. Christian fell in love with Ana at first sight and called her every day after she left to continue her trip to Spain. When she returned to London, Ana enrolled herself in the Goethe Institute to learn German in order to be able to communicate with Christian, who invited Ana to Berlin. As Ana had never been to Berlin before, she accepted. At that time, she was earning seven pounds and fifty shillings a week but managed to travel and still pay for her share of the flat. When she arrived in Berlin, Christian introduced Ana to his parents, who received her very warmly. Christian lived with his autistic brother in a flat he took Ana to see as well. Without Ana's knowledge, Christian had already told his parents about his intention to marry Ana, and his parents had sent out invitations for Christian's engagement party and had asked Christian to go to a jeweler to buy an engagement ring for

Ana. Ana could not back out as her name and Christian's were written on the engagement card. Ana had to go back to London to give up her flat and went back to Berlin. At the insistence of Christian's parents, she enrolled herself at the Goethe Institute for three months to study German. At that time, the government policy was to encourage younger people to migrate to Germany, and as an incentive, each couple was given DM 1,500 to settle down in Berlin in order to compensate for the older generation. However, racial discrimination was still prevalent and it was difficult for Ana to get a flat to stay in. At the same time, in the midst of moving to Berlin, Ana lost her birth certificate. But luckily for her, the strict female officer who was usually on duty was on leave and she managed to get permission to marry Christian from a male officer. As her usual practice, Ana did not invite her family or friends to her impending wedding except for one American girl from her German class in order to be her witness. She wore a white summer coat over a normal dress and flowers in her hair. The ceremony was done in German and luckily for her American friend, she only had to say "Ja" as she could not answer in German. It was a simple ceremony as none of her friends, even if she invited them, would want to come to Berlin in those days. She recalled that when told that she could get the flat she applied for at the ceremony, she excitedly threw her wedding bouquet at the registrar. It was quite unusual, as the registrar said in his thirty years of working there he had never before received a wedding bouquet.

Ana became pregnant immediately at twenty-nine years old and she met many Malay girls from her country married to German men. She found out that German men treated their women kindly and were not selfish. Christian worked long hours at his father's art gallery, and her father-in-law would drive her to the doctor whenever Ana felt nauseous while Christian was at work. At first she found her mother-in-law to be domineering and old-fashioned, but after being able to communicate with her they began to love each other. Her mother-in-law would buy her jar food and feed her well while she was pregnant. Mark was born while Christian was at the art gallery working.

At the beginning of their married life, they got on well, and Ana would encourage Christian to take a holiday to the east on his own from his heavy work schedule. Christian went to Thailand alone the first time and came to resume his normal working life. However, after his second trip to Thailand alone, he came back a different man. Ana noticed that he was not himself and one day she noticed a chain round his neck. Christian also received a letter from a girl in Thailand asking for money to help her sick grandparents. In the meantime, Ana was not happy in Berlin and was always sick. One day, after a consultation with her doctor, she was advised to go back to London. She then asked Christian to file for a divorce. Christian was not ready for a divorce and often got drunk when unhappy, and agreed to pay one thousand marks in order to delay the divorce. The divorce was cancelled and they went on for another two years until they both decided on a mutual divorce after Christian went to Taiwan for a business meeting and met a Taiwanese girl called Chin, whom Ana later befriended. There was no money settlement, but Christian gave the art gallery to Ana to take over and it was doing well. However, Ana's heart was in London and she decided to take her son Mark to London with her as German law gave priority to the mother, even though at first her parents-in-law wanted to fight for custody of their grandson Mark.

Back in London, it was easy to get jobs then as one could, in those days in the 1960s, change jobs like changing clothes. After her earlier modelling stint with the BBC, she managed to get a job as a secretary. She had also tried acting in a movie produced by BBC as a Malaysian student earlier on. With her son with her, she bought a little house at Acton, and Mark finished his schooling there. Being a lover of roses, she planted many different species of roses as her hobby besides indulging herself with her social life. Coincidentally, at that time, her relatives from home kept coming to London and she was kept busy socializing with them. She became their tour guide and frequented the favorite spots of the rich and famous, besides travelling with them as part of their entourage. Life was good and exciting, and her preoccupation with her newly reunited relatives left her hardly any time to pursue any romantic inclination in her life. She followed her royal sister everywhere and recalled having a fabulous time visiting Nice, Cannes, Juan Le Pins, and Geneva in Switzerland, staying at the best hotels. That was how her love affair with France began and she craved to live in France as she found the language and the people fascinating. She returned to Paris many times later on her own or with friends. On recollection, she said there was not a famous restaurant or hotel or club in London that she had not been to with her relatives, and the good life spoiled her so much so that she did not need a man to take her to those nice places.

She traveled extensively with friends or relatives and never regretted her divorce from Christian as she said they were not compatible. While she was very sociable and loved meeting people, Christian was very bookish. And whenever they were on holiday together, she ended up alone, chatting with various people. They still remain friends and call each other from time to time. Ana now lives alone in her one-bedroom apartment as Mark left London to settle down in Berlin with his wife of French origin and two beautiful daughters. Life is not as exciting as before as most of her relatives stopped coming to London and some of her friends have returned home. She is now a British citizen and twice her attempts to live in Malaysia failed as she realized that the lifestyle did not suit her. She still sees some friends from her homeland who now reside in the UK, and from time to time visits her son and her two granddaughters, whom she adores. When I asked this adventurous lady if she regretted making her life in London, she replied, "No. My life is destined here." She has enjoyed fifty years of her life in this vibrant city being alone. She has always been alone, being an only child, and had lived her life alone, growing up with just her mother. This is her destiny, she said.

"Where lies the land to which the ship would go?
Far, far ahead, is all her seamen know
And where the land she travels from?
Away, far, far behind, is all that they can say."
—Arthur Hugh Clough

The young Ana

Raihana with son Mark in Berlin

Berlin in winter

Raihana with Mark and grandchildren

Marbella in Summer

Puerto Banus

Restaurant in Colahonda

Colahonda , Malaga

RESTAURANT IN PUERTO BANUS

Colahonda , Malaga

Chapter 9

(A) A Blessed Life: Marie

When I first met Marie, she was working for the managing director of a British international company. We were officemates, and I would always remember her as she displayed energy and adventure. Always happy-go-lucky and smiling, she was always on the go, which was quite unusual for a Chinese girl. And her western mannerisms were quite the opposite of the Hainan Chinese that I was used to seeing. She moved fast in her petite frame and greeted everyone as she passed. I did not see her again, nor was in touch with her as we were from different planets and lifestyles I thought, until thirty years later when we were brought together by a mutual friend in London. I was going to meet a Mrs. Soskin, a Malaysian girl married to a *Mat Salleh*, a term used by Malaysians for a westerner. It came as a pleasant surprise to me when Mrs. Soskin turned out to be my long-lost friend from our old office, and we quickly caught up with each other's lives. Marie apparently was in her second marriage, to an Englishman of Russian descent. Her first marriage to a Frenchman gave her a girl called Loo Ming, while with her present marriage she had a fourteen-year-old boy named Paul. As we were having roast beef and Yorkshire pudding at a little hotel at Wrights Lane in the lovely district of High Kensington, Marie rattled on about her life and asked me in between about my life, which in comparison was very uneventful. While she had "globetrotted" from her motherland to Europe and Hawaii during her younger days till now, I am still tied to my homeland, only escaping from the routine lifestyle every few months for a holiday in order to liberate myself and my way of thinking. Marie was managing her little shop at Bute Street in Kensington where she kept a *pied-à-terre* upstairs while managing the boutique downstairs, selling women's clothing and accessories she bought in from Paris. It was more of a hobby for her as her main income was from property investments, having bought and sold properties at a young age. While she was working at Rothmans in Kuala Lumpur, she had bought a little bungalow in Port Dickson and rented it out to the staff at Rothmans for their weekend getaways. With her keen business acumen, she started investing in properties even during her days working with Pan American Airways, picking up small investments in Paris and London when the prices at that time in the sixties were affordable and mortgages were easy to get for first-time investors.

Born Lai Chong Gaik and later baptized Marie-Joan, she was born of Chinese parents from Malaysia. She must have been a hyperactive child, because when I met her she appeared to always be on the move, living life to the fullest. She moved fast, talked fast, and took an interest in everything around her to the point of appearing curious about things, qualities that got her ahead and helped her accomplish things at a young age. Her petite frame never aged throughout the years, and after living in France for many years, she has managed to achieve the "chic" French appearance.

At seventeen years of age, she and her brother left for England, where she pursued a degree in business administration in Chiswick for four years. It was after completing her degree in England that she returned home and started to work in a British tobacco company. She became the personal assistant to the vice president, who was an Englishman from Yorkshire, but found the job too dull for her lively personality. She left again for England and joined Pan American Airways as a stewardess, and later was promoted to purser and finally as an inflight director. Working for an American company gave her many opportunities to be promoted until eventually she was made the vice president of the International Union of Flight Attendants. Since her travelling days, she had always been fascinated by Paris and alternated her stay between London and Paris during her leave of absence period or LOA, which normally occurred between October and April. While traveling between Paris and London, she met her first husband, a Frenchman. Later they moved to Honolulu, where she continued working for the airline as a recruiter while her husband worked at the House of Adler as a diamond dealer. Marie always had a penchant for business and started building her property portfolio from a young age. She bought her first flat in Paris, as in those days mortgages were easy to get and her salary at Pan Am enabled her to get mortgages in order to buy properties. In 1980, at the age of thirty, she became the owner of a boutique at her own premises in South Kensington, which she called Marie Soskin, adopting the name of her second husband, Soskin. She invested in another building where she set up another shop called Marie Soskin Bis, meaning Marie Soskin Again. Her third shop was called Emmesse, pronounced MS, which was her initials. It was at Draycott Avenue, a nice London address where she had Imran Khan, the Pakistani cricketer, as her top-floor neighbor with whom she regularly shared meals. Her buying and selling properties became an addictive hobby, and she has lived in many parts of London through her investments until she eventually decided to spend time in the southern region of France near the famous Cote D'Azur. She and husband Nikolas decided to reside in the beautiful countryside in Grasse, famous for its perfume making, in a typical French farmhouse. Nikolas enjoyed tending to their hectares of land, driving his own tractor, after his retirement as a banker in London. It was at her lovely farmhouse on a hill overlooking the French countryside that she decorated with her good taste, with books all over the place, over a lunch of Malaysian chicken curry and rice prepared by her Malaysian Chinese housekeeper, that I persuaded Marie to write me her story in her own words.

"My life began in Port Swettenham in Klang on 31 May, sometime in the last century. My father came from Hainan from a historical landowner dynasty dating back to 1326. Our pioneer forebears were two brothers from the Province of Yunan who came to settle in Hainan in 1326. At the age of forty-six, my father married my mother, who was only nineteen at the time, and she bore him four children, my three brothers and myself. After obtaining my Senior Cambridge at the Convent of the Holy Infant Jesus, I was sent off to England to pick up a couple of A levels alongside a business administration course at the West London College and Chiswick Polytechnic, all arranged by the British Council in Kuala Lumpur. I rented a room from a charming, prim and proper, old English spinster who took a very responsible attitude towards my welfare and introduced me to a typical and austere British lifestyle.

"London in the sixties was experiencing the beginning of the hippy revolution which would spread over the Western world as a reaction to the hardship of the Second World War and post war years. The Beatles and Rolling Stones led the music revolution, Carnaby Street. Barbara Hulanicki (Biba) and Mary Quant were the fashion icons while David Hockney, Patrick Caulfield and Bridget Riley introduced pop art and op-art to the world.

"Night life in the 60s in London revolved around night clubs such as Mark Birley's Annabel's, Robert Mills' The Garrison and The Saddle Club in Mayfair while Aretousa and Raffles opened in the newly fashionable Kings Road.

"For a young Malaysian student, all of this was a wonderful experience, and I partied with other young Malaysians and Singaporeans, many of whom are now important and influential in this region. In those days we were considered "The Privileged Ones"—young and happy, uncomplicated, living in a foreign country. We would earn extra money during the winter holidays by working in shops such as Harrods and Selfridges so as to be able to spend the summer holidays travelling in Europe to France, Italy and Greece. Many other international friendships were made amongst the college students, for example, my friends Princess Mumtaz from Tanzania and Coleen from Rhodesia and Stan Hughes-Roberts from Wales whom we kept in touch with for many years thereafter.

"Towards the end of my student days, after about four years living in London, I enrolled for work experience with the construction company, George Wimpey who were at that time building the Panama Link in Bahrain. It was via this link that I met and got engaged to a Swedish engineer, Anders, from Malmo. He was from an old aristocratic Swedish family and the summer of 1970 was spent in his various family homes in Stockholm, the Lake at Karlstad and Malmo. Life with this family was very warm and formal; for example, we had to dress up almost every evening in formal attire for dinners which consisted of several courses. Before each course, we had to raise our glasses, look into the eyes of the person on our left and say 'skol,' then do the same to the person on the right before we can start eating. Difficult when you are starving, especially for me, being an Asian!

"On returning to Malaysia I was offered a job by WHO as an Administrative Assistant. However, after six months of the intensity of being surrounded by colleagues with multiple PhD's and going through reams of paper on, for example, 'The Eradication of Malaria' and 'Impact of Technological Changes in Rural Inhabitants,' I came to the conclusion that this was not my world. I left to join Rothmans of Pall Mall where I thought life would be more sophisticated and also where I began my longstanding friendship with the author of this book.

"My yearning for adventure had not left me and two years later when I answered an advertisement in *The Straits Times* by Pan American World Airways and was accepted as a flight attendant, my life turned another corner. The first casualty was my engagement, which I felt necessary to break off, although Anders and his family and I remained friends and met several times in Stockholm until he got married and went to live in Chile. The last time I bumped into Anders was in Auckland in New Zealand where he and his wife, Anna, were on holiday and I was on a Pan Am layover. Small world, you can say!

"My flight training took place in Miami, Florida, and when asked where I would like to be based, I chose Pan Am's new base in London. I moved into a flat in fashionable Belgravia above Drones, a very popular and celebrity infested restaurant owned by, amongst others, the actor David Niven. My life in London took a more sophisticated and elegant dimension than my student life in the sixties. In between my flying schedule, I was invited to spend weekends at

English country houses and to attend dinner parties with the London society. I would show up at my host's dinner parties or weekend stays with kilos of golden caviar, obtained at the black market in Tehran on my Pan Am One and Pan Am Two trips. I later realized why I was a popular guest!

"When not in London, which was my home base, I was going places and homes were the Intercontinental Hotels in different cities. I remember in Beirut we would water ski at breakfast at the St. Georges' Hotel, snow ski in the afternoons and frequent The Royal Casino Cabaret in the evenings or nightclubbing at Les Caves and also at St. George's Hotel across the street from the Phoenicia Inter-Continental. Later Les Caves du Roi, when war broke out in the latter seventies, moved to St. Tropez in France. Beirut was called the Paris of the East in those days.

"At this time, Pan Am was offering certain employees the opportunity of a six-month voluntary leave of absence, and so I took the opportunity to go and live in Paris. Shortly on arrival in this beautiful city, I was introduced to one of Paris's most eligible bachelors, the handsome Baron Antoine de Galembert (who had lived in Malaysia in the seventies) and through him I found my first apartment at No.38, Avenue Gabriel, which was his family bastion of several apartments with various family members living at this address. We were next door to the Élysée Palace and were surrounded by many guards. Not needing to be safe, I felt safe. The Matriarch, the Duchess de Galembert, mother of Antoine, took me under her wing and looked after me. Additionally, through an old and well-connected friend from Singapore, the swinging bachelor Etienne, Le Marquis des Roys. I was quickly introduced to the finer side of Parisian life with weekends spent at its night club haunts such as New Jimmy's and Chez Castel and weekends flitting from one chateau to another or a helicopter ride to St. Tropez. Etienne was the most eccentric and colorful personality I had ever met, and besides a career in politics, he was also a successful businessman with interests in Brazil. He started the fashionable and renowned modelling agency called Carrette only because he claimed he enjoyed doing the interviewing. Sadly, he died a couple of years ago, still swinging and enjoying life to the end as a bachelor.

"No sooner was I beginning to enjoy life as a single girl in Paris, I was charmed by one six foot five inches giant compared to my five feet two inches stature, a blond Jewish man, Robert Joffo, whose family owned a chain of eleven hairdressing and beauty salons in Paris as well as others in St. Tropez and Val d'Isère, the ski resort. His family history as Jewish immigrants had been portrayed in the bestselling book *Un Sac de Billes* (A Bag of Marbles), which was translated into many languages and made into a film and was and still is an O-level French literature book in schools in the UK and elsewhere. We got married shortly after the meeting and marital life was a dream, divided between Paris and St. Tropez in the summer and Val d'Isère in the winter months. However, maybe because life was so good and easy, we got itchy feet and decided to go and live in Hawaii, where we also wanted our child to be born. Life in Hawaii continued to be a beach with petanque competitions (or boules) on Waikiki, night clubbing and dining at the Diamond Head Hilton and attending lots of dinner parties amongst the French expatriates. Robert became a diamond dealer with the help of a Jewish compatriot, Jacques Adler, a Belgian who owned the House of Adler.

"It was while living in Hawaii and shortly after our daughter Lu Ming was born that a former boyfriend from the seventies, Nikolas Soskin, showed up to find me. Nikolas Soskin was British, an Old Etonian and banker in London whose Russian father, Paul Soskin, had been a well-known film producer. I had first met him when working for Rothmans of Pall Mall in Malaysia in the early seventies while he had been on a business trip to the Far East. I persuaded my husband to move back to Paris, which he did very amicably. After much to-ing and fro-ing between Paris and London over a span of six years, I left my husband to marry Nikolas. By this time, Nick was long divorced and his first wife had got remarried. However, Robert did not make it easy for me to get a divorce quickly, so Nikolas and I flew to Haiti to get a divorce before marrying the very next day. My ex-husband and I remain good friends to this day and through his good-naturedness he has slowly begun to accept Nick and we do see each other whilst in Paris.

"From 1960's London to the 1970's and now the 1980's, we are older now and London life was less frenetic but no less enjoyable. Weekend shooting parties with Nick's friends, a box at the Royal Opera House in Covent Garden and tickets to Wimbledon thanks to his company's perks, lunches at the White's tent at Royal Ascot, all made London life enjoyable. Our son, Paul, was born in 1986, and in 1989, we decided to move to live in the south of France. Paul was first educated at the local French school before going as a boarder to Ashdown House in Sussex, followed by Eton, where he was Cadet Corps with Prince Harry. Eton College in those days was started by King George VI. In order to be able to be accepted into Eton, one must have a family history and be registered in the house list on the waiting list.

"Life in South of France is more relaxing thanks to the good climate and beautiful surroundings. We have made friends from all parts of the world who either live permanently or have holiday homes there. We are more popular than ever with our old friends back in Britain, who enjoy visiting us. I took up golf so as to partner my husband and he complains that I now play better than he does. We are lucky that we live in the vicinity of such excellent golf courses like the Chateau de Taulane, Cannes Mougins and the Royal Mougins. Our local town, Grasse, is the historical centre for the perfume industry and as you walk down the streets of the Old Town, you can smell the aroma of the lavender, roses and other flowers which are used as the base for perfumes.

"It was in 2010, when we were on a visit to Malaysia that we decided to apply for the MM2H programme and spend a substantial part of the year in Malaysia. We now typically spend the winter months in Malaysia, where we play golf, travel within the region, and I am able to spend time with my mother, who is approaching her ninetieth birthday, and divide the summer months between being based in the south of France and visiting family and friends in Paris and London, where we also have pied-à-terres. In Malaysia we live in Bukit Damansara and have a weekend house on the Serendah Golf Resort. We are hoping to build a house on the east coast soon as we love the sea.

"The changes in Malaysia since I lived here as a child are significant. Infrastructure, such as the roads and public transport system have improved tremendously. Public services are efficient and people are so much more civic minded, all of which contribute to making Malaysia a very pleasant place to live. Notwithstanding these changes and improvements, the country has not lost its basic charm and character. We feel welcome both as visitors and as returning citizens. A great many of my friends still live here and many others have returned, like me, after prolonged absences abroad. This adds greatly to the enjoyment of life here for me. Most of my 'Balek Kampong' group of friends and I share a lot of life's joys in common. We have children and grandchildren, we enjoy eating in the favorite haunts and playing golf together. I have sadly lost contact with some old friends but am happy to have made new ones."

Marie, as I know her, is always organizing her life and enjoying life entertaining and being entertained while travelling to enrich her life and knowledge. She has had a pleasurable life and her happy-go-lucky attitude makes her life interesting wherever she decides to be. Although her daughter was born abroad and is married to a westerner, she has managed to inculcate in her Asian values that neither her daughter nor her husband Nick ever feel like foreigners in her motherland. Whenever she and her family are in Malaysia, it feels like coming home, and she has had a blessed life indeed and is the envy of many in our youthful days. She has been blessed with a life of adventure and good fortune in a foreign land. Nevertheless, her ties with her motherland remain with her till today.

Marie in France

THE COUNTRYSIDE

MARIE WITH LOO MING AND PAUL

ENTERTAINING AT HOME

Home in Graz

Chapter 10

HOME IS WHERE THE HEART IS

I walked my Nordic walk around the Lake Gardens around the focal point of Kuala Lumpur where the parliament house and the warriors' monument are situated. Not far is the Selangor Club, a strategic place where every year the celebration for the Independence Day or Hari Merdeka, now Malaysia Day, took place for the past fifty-seven years. Malaya, during the reign of our first Prime Minister Tengku Abdul Rahman, finally got its independence from the British, making us no longer a British colony as a few other third-world countries. The Malaysians rejoice every year on the thirty-first of August.

As we cross each other's paths along the tarred road while absorbing the beauty of the lake, we do greet each other pleasantly as fellow citizens. It does not escape our eyes that one or two walkers had gone through a difficult period during the Second World War, and had lived to a pleasant old age to celebrate yet another year of independence. Some, like me, were the baby boomers of the 1950s and some from the later years who enjoyed the less difficult period compared to what the elder generation had gone through. We smile at each other, ready to begin our first conversation, which could result in a long-term friendship of sharing pleasantries, hobbies, business introductions, and visiting each other's homes during the festive seasons or just reminiscing over old times over breakfast of local favorites: *roti canai, nasi lemak,* and *teh tarik.*

Today, as I reminisce at how time has flown since our first Independence Day in 1957 when I was just a child, the words of our Prime Minister "Merdeka" over Radio Malaya still echo in my ears. As I walk my six thousand steps, breathing in the fresh air of the surrounding greenery along the well-manicured gardens, I feel blessed to be in a place I have been familiar with through most of my life. The different species of plants and the different colors of the hibiscus flower, which was chosen to represent our country, never failed to amaze me as I walk along the tropical nature that form part of my country's vegetation. Although there have been periods of boredom and discontentment and I have felt the need to be away from this inward-looking society, after a long break of gallivanting and photo taking, nothing gives me greater pleasure than to arrive home at the familiar airport and be greeted by the friendly and smiling faces of my countrymen. Their simple mannerisms and eager-to-please attitude, ready to help everyone, including foreigners, is what make them special despite their shortcomings. I grew up in this multiracial society where my next-door neighbor on the right was Chinese and my next-door neighbor to the left was Indian, both Malaysians but having ancestors who migrated from their respective motherlands. The beauty of my country is that we enjoy each other's cuisines, and when we are away in a foreign land, it is good to meet another Malaysian. I guess the same goes for all those people who have made their homes where their heart is.

The End

Printed in the United States
By Bookmasters